Mom and Dad

Xmas 1971.

Susan and Erik

The Gary Cooper Story

THE

GARY COOPER

STORY

BY

George Carpozi Jr.

ARLINGTON HOUSE   *New Rochelle, N.Y.*

Library of Congress Catalog Card Number 79-101954

SBN 87000-075-6

MANUFACTURED IN THE UNITED STATES OF AMERICA

To The Great Legion of Gary Cooper Fans—

TO REMEMBER HIM ALWAYS . . .

Contents

CONTENTS

Acknowledgements

The author is greatly indebted to scores of writers, authors, researchers, historians, and members of the Hollywood film colony for the information and material used in the preparation of this biography on Gary Cooper, one of the most beloved actors of our time. In particular the author wishes to acknowledge aid he received and to thank the following:

Paul Feis, head librarian and supervisor of the Reference Department of the old New York *Journal-American;* the New York Public Library for invaluable source material provided from its Lester Sweyd Collection; Jack J. Podell, editorial director of Macfadden-Bartell Corp., for his kind permission to research the files of *Photoplay* and *Motion Picture* magazines; Pat de Jager, editor of *Photoplay* and to the magazine's writers and contributors: Herb Howe, Inga Arvard, William F. French; Alice Schoninger, editor of *Motion Picture* and to those who contributed reports: Charles Samuels, Jean Ward, Duncan Underhill, Don Camp, Peter Sherwood, Ruth Waterbury; Pete Martin of the *Saturday Evening Post;* Hollywood columnist Louella Parsons and Phyllis Battelle, both of Hearst Headline Service; the late Elsa Maxwell, whose source material in the New York *Journal-American* and in other publications was invaluable in the preparation of this book; Broadway columnist Louis Sobol, movie reviewer Rose Pelswick, society columnist Igor Cassini (Cholly Knickerbocker), the late dean of sports columnists, Bill Corum, and Henry McLemore, all of the New York *Journal-American;* Thomas F. Brady, Sam Zolotow, Val Adams, Thomas M. Pryor, and movie reviewer Bosley Crowther, all of the New York *Times;* Marie Torre, Beth Twiggar, Tex McCrary and Jinx Falkenburg, Hollywood columnist Joe Hyams, and Art Buchwald, all then of the old New York *Herald-Tribune;* Hollywood columnist Sidney Skolsky, Broadway columnist Earl Wilson, Stan Opotowsky, and Irene Thirer, all of the New York *Post;* Hollywood columnist Sheilah Graham, columnist Sidney Fields—who writes "Only Human"—and George McEvoy, all then of the New York *Mirror;* Hollywood columnists

Hedda Hopper (who costarred in an early Coop picture) and Florabel Muir, movie reviewers Kate Cameron and Wanda Hale, Paris correspondent Bernard Valery, society columnist Nancy Randolph, and Julia McCarthy, all of the New York *Daily News;* Norton Mockridge, Edd Johnson, Halsey Raines, and Michael Mok, all then of the New York *World-Telegram & Sun;* Inez Robb, Morton Von Duyke, John Wix, and L. W. Meredith, all then of International News Service (now combined as United Press International); columnist Hal Boyle and Hollywood writer Thomas Bacon of the Associated Press; Richard Gehman in the old *American Weekly;* Louis Berg of *This Week,* and the distinguished author and Hollywood screen writer Adela Rogers St. Johns.

Special thanks to the late Dorothy Kilgallen, whose association with the author on the old *Journal-American* had prompted her to express the wish to "read the finished manuscript of Coop so I can 'plug' it on the jacket." Miss Kilgallen had previously endorsed the author's biography of Marilyn Monroe by saying: "This is a warm, exciting and truthful biography of the screen's most exciting personality by one who really knows her!" Miss Kilgallen was extremely helpful in providing anectodal material about Gary Cooper that appears throughout the book.

The author also found valuable information on Cooper in such publications as *Time, Life, Newsweek,* and *Esquire.*

In the nearly 10 years spent in the preparation and writing of this book, the author also found the personal experiences narrated by persons who knew Coop intimately most helpful. In particular the author wishes to acknowledge the assistance of Nunnally Johnson, Tallulah Bankhead, Joan Crawford, and Nancy Carroll.

A first-person story by Gary Cooper, as told to Leonard Slater, in *McCall's* magazine, also was helpful as source material.

Rogers & Cowan Inc., the public relations firm that handled Coop, also proved helpful in furnishing background on him. The author wishes to express his gratitude in particular to John Friedkin, of the New York office. Thanks also to Renee Leff, of the New York office, and to Warren Cowan and John Foreman, of the West Coast office, and especially to Jack Hirshberg on the Coast for his splendid 22-page biographical sketch and

complete list of motion pictures and leading ladies with whom
Coop played.

To all the officials and aids at Paramount, Columbia, Metro-
Goldwyn-Mayer, and Warner Brothers, and to the "flacks" of
these studios—the author extends heartfelt thanks.

A very special note of gratitude must go to John Pascal, co-
author of the recent Broadway musical smash, *George M,* for his
efforts in research and editorial assistance on this book.

Generous help in the preparation of this book was provided
by Mr. Lee Fischer; Miss Julia M. Hussey; Sam Gilluly, director of the Montana Historical Society; Mrs. Harriett C. Meloy,
acting librarian of the Montana Historical Society; and S. Bob
Riskin.

GEORGE CARPOZI JR.

The Gary Cooper Story

CHAPTER ONE

Tall in the Saddle

Drift back through the decades, through more than thirty years of memory, across a harsh Western prairie to a town called Medicine Bow, a clutch of ramshackle wooden buildings rotting in the cruel Western sun. Step inside the Medicine Bow Saloon and — if you can shield your ears against the honky-tonk tune a seedy piano player is pounding out in the corner — edge over to a tense poker game and kibitz for a while. And listen.

A darkly bearded saddletramp is there, fidgeting in finger-drumming impatience. Dust from the plains crusts his clothes and a hard glint in his eyes tells you clearly he is the villain.

Among the others around the table is a lean, slouching, ruggedly handsome cowboy. He studies his poker hand. He purses his lips and studies some more. He is contemptuously aware of the villain across the table.

The villain's name is Trampas, and he is becoming angry, boiling, uncontrollably angry at the casualness of the

1

thin cowboy across from him. Then . . .

"Bet!" the word roars out. Trampas glares at the object of his rage. "Bet, you son-of-a-b———!"

Still squinting at his cards, the cowpoke drops his hand to his holster, draws his six-shooter, and lazily places his gun hand on the scarred tabletop. Only then does he care to look at Trampas.

"When you call me that," he drawls in a deep, slow-paced voice, "*smile!*"

The handsome cowboy, of course, is Gary Cooper. Could anyone else have delivered that line and have gotten away with it? Could Cooper have said anything else?

It was spoken in a picture called *The Virginian*, in 1929. It was a line as corny as a Sunday picnic in Topeka but it thrilled the moviegoer of that day in the Roaring Twenties —and all the days afterward into the atomic and space ages. Despite the endless procession of mass-produced cactus heroes who rode herd over the Western ranges on the movie screens for nearly four generations, despite the crooning cowhands, the galloping posses, the reverberating hoofbeats, and despite the gunfire, the roundups, the fading sunsets, and the thousand-and-one other memorable scenes that characterize celluloid epics of the West, one man stood so tall in the saddle and embodied all that is right and proper that he reigned unchallenged as the true Man of the West.

Gary Cooper was that man.

For 36 years, the tall, drawling Gary Cooper gave America and the world the image of the rugged frontiersman in a continuous, unbroken stream of movies. And yet, in his long and memorable career, which incredibly spanned nearly four decades, the lithe, lanky, leathery-faced sagebrush hero had immortalized himself with roles that, paradoxically, were as diversified as those essayed by most of his peers.

All the world will remember Coop as the unhurried hero, the gangling, inarticulate champion of the just and the good, incorruptible, endearingly shy, but in the end quite willing and always capable of taking matters into his own hands with a fast gun or a thundering smash to the jaw. Yet the image doesn't conform precisely to the facts.

In nearly 100 films over the remarkable period of time he reigned unchallenged as the Man of The West — from the mute days before Vitaphone to the era of wide, wide panoramic screen and stereophonic sound — Gary Cooper actually had portrayed an awesomely broad spectrum of characters.

When he played opposite Audrey Hepburn in *Love in the Afternoon*, Gary Cooper was a sophisticate on the prowl for a young enchantress many years his junior; in Ayn Rand's *The Fountainhead*, Coop portrayed an architect in the spirit of Frank Lloyd Wright; in *Bright Leaf* he grew rich on tobacco, married an aristocrat who almost ruined him, and was loved by a bawdy house madam with a heart of gold.

Nor was this the extent of his versatility.

He elicited admiration as the quiet, dignified Robert Jordan, an American fighting with the republican forces during the Spanish Civil War, in *For Whom the Bell Tolls*, the film taken from the book by Coop's friend and fellow outdoorsman, Ernest Hemingway.

Earlier in his career Coop had starred in Hemingway's *A Farewell to Arms*, successfully imparting still another image — an American ambulance corps officer in Italy who first mistakes Helen Hayes for a scarlet woman, then falls in love with her in the classic style of the romantic hero. Again, in another sensitive love story, du Maurier's *Peter Ibbetson*, Coop showed his versatility by portraying the romantic hero loving Ann Harding in a dream world after being separated from her in life.

On and on it went in the fabulous movie career of Gary Cooper — the White Knight in *Alice in Wonderland*, a distinguished professor in *Ball of Fire*, where he researched the letter "S" while editing an encyclopedia. A task, incidentally, that became infinitely simpler after he met Barbara Stanwyck, playing a boogie-woogie stripteaser named Sugarbush O'Shea.

Through it all, Gary Cooper lived and worked in a frenzy of Hollywood drum-beating that perpetually pounded out prose about his "naturalness." Press agents loved to point out that his ability was most apparent only when he played characters tailored to his measure, spoke only lines written to his size, lines he found believable, lines he could live with.

He agreed with them.

If it is true that Coop played himself, then, as a consequence of the inordinate range of movie roles he had performed, one must ask, "Which self was Gary Cooper playing?"

Actually, the answer is imbedded in the cold statistics of box-office returns. When Coop the actor played chiefly his real self, the towering, taciturn man, shy, kind, down-to-earth, loveable, and straitlaced, he always was a hit. When he didn't, his movie public regretfully let him know by the number of seats they left vacant in the nation's theaters.

To America, to the world, Coop personified the American dream of how a hero should act and look — strong, courageous, simple, forthright, quiet, but always able to overcome a villain with gun or fists.

While Coop also could be at home in a sophisticated romp in which elegant ladies dripped mink and diamonds, his public didn't always give him credit for versatility. In spite of the sweeping scope of his ability, the multitude of roles he played so well, to his fans Gary Cooper remained

basically an indestructible image of The Man of the West
—a man of few words, a man of action, a man who worked
things out in his own mind, a man of honest, sincere purpose ... a *good* man.

When cancer began to ravage his body, when he could
make pictures no more, the image Gary Cooper had
created was solidly intact, well-earned, and richly de-
served in the eyes of millions of fans, friends, and admirers
around the globe. He was an enduring symbol of America,
a legend as deeply entrenched as the folklore of the West,
as pure as the heroic Lou Gehrig he once portrayed, as
beloved as any actor who ever held respected sway over
movie audiences.

The Gary Cooper the public knew best was a Galahad,
on horseback and off, shy with women yet not unknowing.
His image was the sum of the vast, overwhelming majority
of his roles — and his publicity.

But perhaps image is not precisely the word, for an
image denies reality. The truth is, despite the endless
reams of publicity Hollywood cranked out in an effort to
associate the Gary Cooper of the screen with the Gary
Cooper of real life, this was one of the very few times the
cinema city flacks were telling it straight.

The man on the screen was a duplicate of the Gary
Cooper of real life, and no episode out of Coop's career
supports this image more strongly than the one that occurred in a London restaurant while Gary was shooting a
picture in England.

Coop had finished his meal, paid his check, and began
to leave. But as he passed a table occupied by three young
men, a sarcastic thrust caught him off guard in a moment
when the other patrons were politely smiling at him in
recognition.

"Oh, look, chaps," he heard one of the three comment

with ill-concealed malice, "a real live movie star."

Big Coop strolled over to the table, leaned his 6 feet, 2¾-inch frame on the table and stared hard at the young man, ignoring his seconds. Coop's jaw tensed for several seconds of deafening silence, and then he drawled in his deep, slow-paced voice:

"Stand up when you say that, stranger."

The youth's blood drained from his face and he croaked out a hasty, "Sorry, old man." Coop turned and shuffled out the door into the London streets. But he might just as well have been walking into a Western sunset. He had silenced another Trampas.

Gary Cooper believed in his heart that the secret of his long success on the screen was "naturalness."

"It's a hard thing for a man to talk about," he would say, "but I guess it boils down to this. You find out what people expect from your type of character, and then give them what they want. That way, an actor never seems unnatural or affected no matter what role he plays.

"Ever since I have been able to pick my own roles, I have refused to do a movie which didn't excite me. I figure that if it excites me — I'm a very ordinary, average guy — it will at least interest most other people. If you're interested in what you're playing, and the audience is interested, too, you can't help but create a feeling of naturalness."

Coop's appearances in films left the universal impression that he was indeed easygoing, casual, and, perhaps, not trying too hard to act. Being himself, it might have seemed, was a lazy man's way of acting through reel after reel; there was no need to sweat over acting techniques since he had the built-in qualities of the characters he portrayed.

But Gary Cooper never regarded his work as a lark, and he never breezed through it with the casualness he seemingly displayed before audiences. He worked hard at it from the very beginning, for Coop viewed his work with the cold objectivity of a true professional.

His feeling was that a topnotcher must not relax lest a newcomer take over. He never relaxed.

"A newcomer who scores a hit has it much easier," Coop insisted. "The reviewers like to make their own discoveries and the newcomer has publicity handed to him. The established star is always on the spot. People expect him to be good, and if he isn't — watch out!"

The dominant public concept of Coop only partially reflected the man. For all of the utterances of "yup" and "nope" that have been associated with his lifetime of movie work, no one loathed those legendary expressions more than Coop. Actually, he had not mouthed those words in a movie in decades — if ever — and yet they became legends associated with Coop. His suspicion was that the whole thing snowballed from a chance phrase once turned by an imaginative studio press agent.

Yet no one who has ever seen Coop on screen can deny that he used a monosyllabic vocabulary that endeared him to everyone. It once prompted Carl Sandburg to call him "one of the most beloved illiterates this country has ever known."

Life magazine in 1950 summed up Gary Cooper in a rare editorial tribute on the occasion of his 25th anniversary as a film star:

"Oh, to look at Gary Cooper. There's a fellow who doesn't need a Brooks Brothers suit, shoulder pads, a button-down shirt, a hand-painted tie or even a shoeshine. Just give him a pair of tight-fitting pants for his legs to strain against, an old shirt and vest to keep his chest expansion within bounds, a black string tie to hide his Adam's apple, and a dusty pair of boots to die in.

"He'll go riding away tree-tall and grim, looking the way a man should look, a friend to the righteous, a hero to children, and a flytrap to women. Doesn't have to say a word. Doesn't even have to smile. One look at Gary Cooper and the weak take heart, the villains take to cover and the women faint."

Coop grinned at this. Yet it was more than the total of his screen characterizations. In everything Coop did, there was always a great big hunk of Gary Cooper there for all to see and thrill.

Across nearly 40 years of moviemaking, millions went to the theater just to watch Gary Cooper, not in any old role but in parts that he wanted to do. For Cooper, show business giant that he was, an actor's actor whose pictures grossed more than $200,000,000, felt a deep and abiding obligation to the public that had made him its idol. He never lent his efforts to the portrayal of a character that could have a bad influence on his audiences — especially on the young.

"Criminals are kids — regardless of their age," Cooper maintained. "We have juvenile delinquents of 10, 12, and 45. They're all juveniles. They never appraise the odds against them. And when they see a show they try to identify with the hero.

"If the hero is a heel — the influence can be dangerous. Kids get too steady a diet of violence today. It is justified in my mind only if the good guy overcomes tremendous odds to lick the bad guy."

This was Gary Cooper always and forever on the movie screen — a good guy who overcame the big odds to take over the bad guy.

His roles may not have been precisely tailored to represent the common man in terms of average income, average education, or average tastes, but they were in a very real sense the representation of common aspirations — they projected an ideal with which most men and boys wanted to associate themselves.

What was this ideal of the average man?

"His strength is as the strength of ten because his heart is pure," laughed Coop. "He is no handsome knight in shining armor, but he is a right guy. A right guy."

That was Gary Cooper right to the end — a right guy.

Whether in the dusty wardrobe of the sagebrush or in city-slicker attire, Coop was St. George wrestling the dragon of evil, overcoming forbidding odds, and in the end winning out and becoming once again "a friend to the righteous, a hero to children, and a flytrap to women."

He was shy yet fierce. He was sheepish yet valiant. He was reluctant yet perceptive. He was pure yet worldly.

He was Everyman.

No man, woman, or child who has thrilled to a Gary Cooper movie will ever forget him.

You can see him now — standing in the sunset on the lonely trail. He has just leaned down to fold the villain's hands gently across his bullet-riddled chest. He begs repose for the soul of this incorrigible outlaw he has just slain in self-defense. The righteous have won again.

Now he stands tall and straight, a wisp of hair dangling over his eye. His sealed lips part ever so slightly to blow the hair away. He mops his brow, straightens his hat, and takes the reins to walk his "hoss" away to the rim of the nearby hill into the setting sun as the background music rises to a crescendo.

Gary Cooper fades out. The long, lean figure, the craggy, inscrutable face, the monosyllabic voice with its warm drawl is gone.

The end.

In films and in life itself, Gary Cooper is gone. But his

spirit and his image will live on — tall in the saddle, tall in memory, tall in the hearts of all who knew and loved him.

The following chapters will recreate the image of Gary Cooper in all its glory, from its beginning, to live on as the biography of a man whom no one will be able to replace in our time.

CHAPTER TWO

A Hell-Roarin'
Mining Town

Picture a tall, lanky, somewhat knock-kneed youth of fourteen dragging himself home, blood gushing from an assortment of cuts on his chin, nose, and cheeks, and his sedate clothes, the very best of English duds, tattered.

You are looking at Frank James Cooper, son of a Montana Supreme Court justice. Hardly what you'd expect the offspring of a distinguished jurist to look like, even if the year is 1915 and the setting is Helena, capital of Montana, not many years removed from its hellfire and brimstone days as a booming and blustery mining town.

Yet that is the portrait of a boy who would grow up to emblazon his name on the marquees of thousands of theaters across the nation and throughout the world. His name: Gary Cooper.

On this particular day in 1915, Frank Cooper's appalling appearance was not so much his own doing as it was that of his classmates. They just didn't go for the fancy English garb Frank wore to school that day. His mother thought her son should exemplify sartorial elegance, even if the rest of the kids came to school in Levi's, cowboy boots, and ten-gallon hats.

Mrs. Alice Cooper admired dignity and decorum. She had brought her sense of British tradition with her from England, and Helena was a disappointment to her at first and for many years afterward. She found it too rugged, too vulgar, too wild. She didn't like the idea of raising her children in an environment steeped deeply in the traditional rough-and-tumble ways of the Wild West.

Mrs. Cooper had come to America from the shipbuilding town of Gillingham in Kent, shortly after the turn of the century. Her maiden name was Brazier. She had a brother, Alfred, who emigrated to Montana before her, and it was at his urging that she sailed for America and settled in Helena.

Not long afterward, in 1893, she met a fellow Englishman, Charles H. Cooper, a railroad worker in the Northern Pacific's roundhouse in Helena. Cooper hailed from Bedfordshire in England and made his way to America in 1885 when he was 19. He had been a farmer in England and aspired to study law, but he gave up the idea when overtaken with adventurous thoughts of going to America to fight Indians.

In America, Charles Cooper found Indian warfare a fading memory. The famous Last Chance Gulch was now the thriving, rapidly expanding metropolis of Helena, Montana. Once again the thought of pursuing law entered Cooper's head. And while working for the railroad, he enrolled in a small college with that goal in mind.

It was inevitable that, in a community as small as Helena, Charles Cooper would meet Alice Brazier, since both were English. And before long they married.

Their first son was born in 1895. He was named Arthur. Their second son, Frank James Cooper, was born May 7, 1901.

Mr. and Mrs. Cooper were still in the midst of hard times when Frank came into this world, for Cooper had only recently earned his degree and hung out his ATTORNEY AT LAW shingle. But conditions improved rapidly and by the time Frank was nine years old the family fortunes were so good that his father was able to buy a sprawling ranch sixty miles north of Helena.

"Dad bought the ranch for Arthur and me to work off steam in the summer," Cooper related years later. His memories of the ranch always remained vivid and clear.

The ranch, named the Seven-Bar-Nine, was a wide plateau in the Missouri River gorge, a rich, flat, fertile area resembling the Great Plains further to the east. But the pancake topography of the land quickly disappeared there at the foothills to the Rocky Mountains and the main Continental Divide. Along the gorge, the Northern Pacific ran a single-track branch line, and on a signal from the Coopers the train would stop to let them on or off.

"We had fast, convenient transportation from Helena to Dad's ranch," Coop remembered. "But that was only when we went on the train. If we decided to hitch up the horse to the wagon, it was a trip that took a long day — and put the nag out of commission for a week."

Today, of course, it's a little over an hour by car, and the old house which stood on the ranch is still there. In 1957, Coop was urged by *Look* magazine to return to his native state for a two-week tour of reminiscences.

"I was able to walk around the old house blindfolded," Gary said. "It didn't seem to have changed except that it appeared smaller than I remembered it. It brought back a lot of memories about what a little shot I was."

Coop's life on the ranch didn't really begin until his teens. Before then, he'd had very little opportunity to orient himself to range life or to work off steam as his father had hoped.

In town, the Coopers lived in a large, ten-room red-brick house, somewhat resembling an English castle, modified in part by a squared-off look that tended to give it an appearance of a small fortress. It was situated on Eleventh Avenue, behind Last Chance Gulch, which was the name retained for the main street when the town was renamed Helena.

Along that main drag, saloons were as plentiful as the gold nuggets that had covered the territory's creek and stream bottoms, before prospectors panned them completely bare.

The gold strike, in 1864, launched Last Chance Gulch on its way; it became the territorial capital in 1881. But by then the gold ore was completely exhausted. The settlers then turned to silver mining, which gave the town renewed prosperity, and later to lead and zinc mining. But through it all, ranching, cattle breeding, and farming grew immensely in the rich agricultural area known as Prickley Pear, or Helena Valley.

On Saturday afternoons Helena became a gathering place for all the ranchers, miners, and cowhands. What occurred then every Saturday afternoon back early in the century was much like the scenes depicted in Western movies. Saloon doors would swing open and drunken brawlers would roll out into the street in bloody combat. The sheriff would rush into the act, break up the fight, and send the beaten battlers home.

And Frank James Cooper?

He'd be right in the thick of things, watching the brawl with all the delight and pleasure a youngster of his age could corral over such excitement. And if a cussword or two happened to be uttered by the combatants, how could Frank help picking it up?

Frank occasionally dropped a cussword or two in his mother's presence — causing Alice Brazier Cooper finally to throw up her hands and declare to her husband:

"Charles, I'm taking the boys to England."

Mr. Cooper had to agree that was the best move. And so Mrs. Cooper packed, gathered her children, and headed for England, leaving behind her husband to carry on his law practice.

After a summer on the Cooper farm in Bedfordshire, Mrs. Cooper, pleased with the improvement in her sons, brought them back to Montana. Almost at once, Arthur and Frank reverted to character — the character of the Wild West. So the following summer they again returned to England. This time Mrs. Cooper forced her husband to take his first vacation and come along.

Again, the children seemed improved to Mrs. Cooper. And for good reason. There were no mud flats, no Last Chance Gulch, no creeks, no wide-open spaces in which to run wild. The charm of the English countryside, the quiet manners of English playmates restricted Frank's and Arthur's escapades. The quiet, subdued life they led made them appear suitably refined.

"We must keep the boys in England," Mrs. Cooper told her husband. "Let me put them in school here so at least they can get a good English education."

Justice Cooper consented.

Mrs. Cooper enrolled Frank and Arthur at Dunstable, a public school their father had attended.

Coop's first day in class was miserable.

"Mr. Cooper, haven't you studied Latin?" asked the headmaster.

Frank looked at the headmaster with a "what's that" expression.

"And what of Shakespeare, how much have you had?"

Well, at least Coop had heard about Shakespeare from his father — but that's as close as he'd come to the bard.

"Would I be wasting my time if I asked whether you've studied French or algebra or, let us say, English history, or geography? . . ."

"I don't know very much, do I?" Coop taunted the head-master.

The headmaster had his work cut out for him. He arranged special sessions with a teacher to bring young Frank up to standard. The headmaster also tried to make Coop feel at home, but it wasn't easy. To catch up with all the studies he lacked, Frank had to stay late in school, and at home his nose was fixed to the scholar's grindstone. But, in time, it all paid off.

After three years, he had learned to speak French, at least knew what Latin was, and had acquired a veneer of English culture and refinement. He even spoke with an English accent of sorts. But he also managed to teach his classmates some Americanisms. Years later, at a class reunion, his classmates' accepted greeting was "Howdy, stranger!"

The headmaster's progress in transforming Coop into a fine little British gentleman was rudely and shockingly set back one day just when he was certain he had succeeded with the boy.

A cockney newsboy insulted young Cooper about the school cap he was wearing.

Coop's even disposition boiled into anger. The lanky youth was now as fast with his fists as a wildcat with its claws.

"I am going to knock your ass off," Coop announced to

the towny, employing the broad "A" which had now become a fixture in his vocabulary.

He then proceeded to do a bunkhouse special on the newsboy, hitting him with fists, elbows — and a bit of the old knee. The street arab was bewildered, yet it was nothing compared with the shock registered at old Dunstable.

"We beg you to remove your son from our school," wrote the headmaster to Mrs. Cooper at the farm in Bedfordshire. "He has quite exceeded the limits of his welcome here."

Mrs. Cooper conveyed the bad news home to her husband in Montana, who sent the fare for the family's return. Coop, his mother and brother returned home to the sagebrush of Montana.

"Imagine," the boy complained to his father, "those little snobs at Dunstable told me, 'You shouldn't fight newsboys. You might get your hands dirty.' As far as I'm concerned they're all a bunch of stinkers."

Young Coop and Arthur were pleasantly surprised on their return home to find their father had taken a more active interest in the ranch he had bought some years before. Actually, the elder Cooper had a soft spot in his heart for a spread of his own, because in England he had been raised on a farm.

So, when the boys arrived in the summer of 1915, they found the ranch bustling with activity. Instead of a few scrub cows, some broken-down mares, and a mean bull that used to terrify the boys, they found five hundred head of heifers roaming the ranch, along with two blue-ribbon Texas Hereford bulls.

But it was not easygoing when the boys got to the ranch. A heavy rainstorm that had lasted for days caused tremendous floods which inundated the land and washed away the Northern Pacific's branch line along the gorge.

While Mr. Cooper fretted over the losses, Frank found occasion to enjoy the catastrophe. Let Coop tell it in one of his favorite boyhood yarns:

"To fix up the railroad in our section, the Northern Pacific brought in a bunch of Turks. These colorful people wore fantastic costumes with red fezzes and carried daggers or knives. None of them spoke English, but in spite of that, when they sat around on their haunches telling stories after sunset, I sat by and watched.

"We had a clear mountain spring on our ranch, 3½ feet deep. It was set right in the shade of aspens, nice and cool. The Turks asked permission to cool their beer in our spring and there were usually about 24 cases in it at a time. Of course, I had never tasted beer before, but one evening they offered me some, and I didn't know how potent it was until I got up to ride home to the ranch. I couldn't understand what was the matter with me when I wove back and forth; but the look on mother's face when I entered the house made me very much aware of the fact that something was dreadfully wrong. However, I didn't get a spanking."

Coop forgot to add that his mother was almost ready to yank her boys back to England once again — except that there wasn't enough time. School was about to start for the fall, so the boys were taken back to Helena.

The English duds they'd brought with them after their three years abroad came out of the closet for the boys — but the sartorial example Frank and Arthur had started out to set at their mother's insistence quickly backfired. Mrs. Cooper knew her sons would have to go back to Western attire when they returned home from school with their clothes in shreds and their bodies quite pummeled.

"At least we didn't run out on the fight when the kids started to rib us about our duds," Coop laughed.

Coop's troubles in school were not only with his class-mates. His principal didn't consider the Latin, French, and Shakespearean studies offered at Dunstable as fulfillment of the curriculum requirements at Helena.

Coop was slapped back into the sixth grade.

Days on the Seven-Bar-Nine

▌▐▐▌

"When he was a boy Frank would go off into the hills, walking or shooting, with the Indian boys. . . . They were the children of the Indians who worked for us and they were about Frank's age. Those Indians never talked much — and Frank would spend hours with them without speaking a word. . . ."

This is how Mrs. Alice Cooper put it when she was asked how her son came to be known as a swell guy who just didn't talk much.

But the old chestnut about action speaking louder than words never applied more perfectly than in Frank Cooper's case, even as a young man on his father's Seven-Bar-Nine ranch.

One of the Indian youths, named White Face, was especially friendly with Frank. One day Frank and White Face sat on a corral fence for hours just gaping out at the breathless scenery beyond the flat where the magnificent Grand Tetons begin to rise 7,000 feet into the bright blue Montana sky.

"Like to climb that mountain?" Coop asked finally, breaking the drought of silence. He pointed to Eagle Rock which rose to a modest 2,000 feet above the Cooper ranch. It was one of the shorter peaks in the Grand Teton range.

"Me too scared," replied the young Indian.

"Me, too," Coop put in.

There was another long period of silence.

"How about a little wrestlin'?" Frank inquired to interrupt the quiet again.

"Me wrestle," agreed White Face.

Coop suggested they each put up something they valued highly as a prize for the winner. Frank offered his leather boots.

"What I give?" asked White Face.

Coop glanced down at the old battered oversized leather chaps the youth was wearing. He had gotten them from a cowhand. Coop had no chaps of his own.

"How about those?" Frank asked, pointing to the chaps.

"Sure," said White Face, shrugging.

It took Frank a few seconds to pin the young brave to the ground — and the chaps were his.

Coop by now was over 6 feet tall. He had grown a phenomenal 13 inches in a year's time. But a lot had happened in that year between 1916 and 1917. World War I had come along and stripped the range of every able-bodied ranch hand. Coop's brother, Arthur, now 21, had gone off to service. The ranch needed looking after — and the job fell to Frank James Cooper and his ma. The American Expeditionary Forces needed beef, and the Seven-Bar-Nine was committed to supply its share from the five hundred head that grazed on its range.

Coop's father? No, he couldn't tend to the ranch. By now Mr. Cooper was a Justice of the Montana Supreme Court and was needed in Helena not only to dispense justice from the bench but also to perform a myriad of services in connection with the war effort. Coop and his mother had to look after the ranch, a difficult task that called for many sacrifices.

One of these was that Frank had to quit school.

"I didn't enjoy the idea," Coop said years later. "I had many thoughts about what I wanted to be, and one of them that stuck in my noodle was the idea that I might become a painter."

That thought occurred to Coop one day when his father took him to the Montana Supreme Court Building in Helena. Walking through the corridors, Frank looked up at the large, impressive painted murals of Western frontier life.

"Gosh, dad," young Coop exclaimed, "these paintings are wonderful. I wish I could paint like that."

Justice Cooper turned to his son and told him there was no reason he couldn't — even though these murals had been done by a master, Charles Russell.

"Son, just remember this. No matter what your aim in life may be, you can make it come true if you will apply yourself. If you want to be a painter, then you can be one. But you must study art and you must paint."

Shortly after that his father bought Frank a set of oils. But Coop's attempts to follow in the footsteps of Charles Russell were inhibited by the war and the call to the ranch.

His days on the ranch were long and tiring. He would get up hours before dawn and put in a sixteen-hour day of backbreaking work that ordinarily required the efforts of a half-dozen ranch hands; at night he barely had enough strength left to crawl into bed.

On rare occasions, as after a roundup when the cattle had been shipped off to Chicago's stockyards, Coop had time to relax. These were the times when he would mosey over to the corral fence and sit atop it, gazing off at the distant mountain ranges, deep in thought, often meditating about his future.

"I used to sit like that for hours," Coop said. "It didn't matter if I was alone or if one of my Indian friends was with me. I had dreams of my own in those days — dreams like climbing Eagle Rock, all of 2,000 feet straight up.

"I could always see it from my house, rain or shine, even at night. It was always there waiting to be climbed. I never did get to it, but the urge was always there."

When Coop revisited the ranch in 1957, he stopped for long minutes looking up at the imposing Eagle Rock.

"Would you like to climb it?" he was asked.

"Yeah, but I don't think it'll let me," Coop replied.

When Coop walked around the house he stopped at one of the windows that faced the barn and recalled another dramatic incident from those difficult years on the ranch.

It was a day shortly after Christmas that Coop was awakened by a strange banging. What he saw startled him. His mother was chopping firewood with an ax. It was at least ten below zero and a recent blizzard had left the ground buried under deep snow.

Furious to see his mother laboring so strenuously, Frank pulled up the window and shouted:

"Ma, what in heaven's name are you trying to prove? You put that ax right down this minute and get into the house. Now hurry on with you."

Mrs. Cooper trudged through the snow into the house to see what the fuss was about.

"If I ever catch you chopping wood again, I'll take you over my knee," Frank said sternly. "So long as I'm around you're going to let me handle those chores. That's an order, ma."

Mrs. Cooper put her arms around her son and buried her face in his chest.

"You're just man enough to carry out your threat," she said with the glint of a tear in her eye. "Frank ... you're a wonderful son. ..."

At sixteen, Coop had sprouted to the full height he would reach in his lifetime — 6 feet, 2 ¾ inches. But all the growth was altitudinal. Leveling off in the neighborhood of 175 pounds, he gained nary an ounce, and that posed the problem of his sporting a silhouette closely resembling a beanstalk.

However, Coop didn't mind. He never gave his height much thought — except when he'd bang his head against the overhang in the bar. The only ambition Frank had after two strenuous years on the ranch was to get away from it. He'd had his fill of ranch life. It wasn't for him.

The winter blizzards and the spring floods that ravaged the ranch were enough to convince Coop that any other pursuit was better than the hard, bitter life of ranching.

Coop looked ahead to the day when the war would end and he could go off in some other endeavor. But what?

Then it came to him. He would follow the desire he had expressed once before — to be an artist. Surely there must be enough money in that field, Coop told himself. Why not give it a try?

When the war was over and ranch hands were again available, Coop went back to high school in Montana.

"My first day in school was almost a nightmare," Coop related. "I found myself with a bunch of kids who were no taller than my bottom rib. I was ready to toss in the towel right then and there."

But Frank found his teacher, Ida W. Davis, sympathetic and understanding.

"We know that you've spent the last couple of years on your parents' ranch," Miss Davis told him. "We have special classes for young men like you who have had to miss some school. We'll see that you get through school without any embarrassment."

Actually, the school had no special classes. But Miss Davis had felt sorry for the tall, gangling youngster, and she went out of her way to make Frank feel that he belonged. And she succeeded, for young Coop finished school with a B average and qualified in the Montana State College entrance exams.

On his 1957 revisit to Montana, Coop made a special effort to find Miss Davis. She had retired years before and was no longer a resident of Helena. Coop hunted high and low and finally located her in Bozeman, Montana.

Tears formed in Coop's eyes when he came face to face with Miss Davis, who was now 77 years old.

"You are the lady responsible in a big way for what has happened to me," he said. "Remember how you helped me give up cowboying and made it possible for me to go to college? You took a lot of us kids out of the mire of indecision and put us on the right road."

Miss Davis smiled, misty-eyed, and bestowed a kiss on Coop's cheek.

"I'm proud of you, Frank," she whispered.

While still in high school, Coop struck up a warm friendship with Harvey Markham, who was about Coop's age. Although Harvey's legs were paralyzed as a result of a childhood attack of polio, he was able to get around and had even learned to drive a Model T Ford equipped with special hand levers for clutch and brake. Harvey drove Coop to and from school each day.

One morning, Harvey and Coop were driving down the steepest hill along their road to school when, suddenly, Harvey couldn't slow the car.

"The brakes," he screamed. "They don't work!"

"I see that," Coop said calmly.

Harvey maintained a cool head as each second brought them closer to disaster. At the bottom of the hill was a cross street. The car had to make the turn there — unless the Ford was rugged enough to tangle with the steep face of a small mountain.

Harvey decided at once to negotiate the turn — if he could.

"Hold on!" shouted Harvey. "I'm gonna try like hell."

"I'm with you, Harvey," Coop said, confident of his friend's hand behind the wheel.

But the corner was too much for the Ford. It overturned, and its occupants, fortunately, were thrown clear. Harvey escaped with a few bruises and minor cuts. Coop also seemed to have gotten off with only scrapes and scratches — until he tried to get to his feet.

"Oh!" he moaned, "my hip's killing me!"

Limping all the way to his family doctor, Frank submitted to an examination and was told he had suffered nothing more serious than a torn ligament in his hip.

"Stay in bed until it feels better," the doctor advised. "Then get up and exercise your hip. Get out of bed as soon as you can and hop on a horse. Riding is the best therapy I can prescribe for a torn ligament."

There's a sequel to this medical opinion in a later chapter.

Coop followed the doctor's advice and went to his father's ranch to convalesce — in the saddle.

"It killed me just to get on the horse," Coop related years later when he told the story to interviewers. "But who was I to argue with medical science? If the doctor said riding was going to cure my hip, that was good enough for me."

During this period when Coop took to the saddle, he was forced to favor his "sore muscles." So Gary developed trick ways of keeping on his mount so that he wouldn't feel the pain. Coop always maintained that this enabled him to ride better than ever before, because it gave him a sixth sense on horseback; by anticipating every move his mount was going to make, Coop became an expert rider — almost as good as his close friend and boyhood hero, Jay "Slim" Talbot, a tall, slender young man greatly resembling Coop in looks and build.

In fact, this resemblance was to figure strongly in Talbot's future, as we'll learn later.

While Coop and Talbot had seen each other often as youngsters, the war had separated them; and after peace came, Slim Talbot went off to become a top-flight rodeo rider. But destiny would bring Coop and Talbot together a few years later under the most unlikely circumstances, in what would be the turning point of Coop's life.

During his period of long convalescence, Coop found solace in the wilderness beyond the ranch, in the mountain foothills beneath the imposing background of the Grand Tetons where he would sit for hours and commune with nature. There, in the absolute quiet of the virgin mountain woodlands, where the only sounds were the rustling of the leaves on the trees and the occasional call of a wild animal, Coop rediscovered the beauties of the rustic West.

"I had time to think," Coop said, "and my thoughts always went back to those murals in the courthouse. If Russell could do it, I said to myself, why can't I?"

Why, indeed. And with that attitude, Coop returned to continue the schooling that had been interrupted by his accident. His hip was mended now.

With Miss Davis's continued inspiring help, Coop graduated from high school and enrolled in Montana State College as an art major. After several months he found he wasn't getting enough out of the courses. His watercolors and charcoal sketches were, as Coop described them, "on the limp side." So he decided to change schools. He picked Grinnell College in Iowa. The year now was 1921.

At Grinnell, Coop buckled down with an intensity he had never before given his studies. He applied himself diligently, and after class he burned the midnight oil working on special projects.

He finished his freshman year with passing grades in all his courses and with above-average marks in art.

"It began to look as if I had a future at that point," Coop said. "I was greatly encouraged."

But during his sophomore year Coop suddenly decided to assess his progress.

"It suddenly occurred to me," he related, "that I might make a surgeon. I thought it would be a great thing. But, alas, I found out from the dean that I had gone too far in my education along nonscientific lines to make the switch. I would have had to start all over — and that was something I didn't want to do."

While in college, Coop was attracted to the idea of trying out for the dramatic club.

"I don't know what made me decide that I could act," Gary said years later when telling of his early interest in the theater. "It was just something that occurred to me at the spur of the moment."

So Coop tried out for the dramatic club.

He didn't make it.

In an interview with Beth Twiggar of the New York *Herald Tribune,* Coop revealed this much for the first time:

"As I remember, I not only stuttered but did it so softly no one could hear me t-two f-feet away!"

Coop didn't blame anyone for his being blackballed. Perhaps because he still saw a career ahead for himself as an artist.

During summer recess, Coop took a job in Yellowstone Park. He worked briefly as a guide, but the pay wasn't as good as it was for the drivers of the buses which hauled tourists up the steep mountainous roads on sightseeing trips. So Coop became a bus jockey.

Someone who remembered those days of the long ago was "Boots" Dunlap, who became a special policeman at the Warner Brothers Studio after Gary had achieved stardom in Hollywood.

"Frank Cooper and I," said Boots, "were gear-jammers together in the park. We drove those buses like wildmen and spieled for the tourists. We'd drive them downhill, down those steep, narrow mountainous roads with the passengers holding on for dear life.

"When Frank came to work at Yellowstone between semesters at Grinnell, we called him 'The Sheik.'

"Frank was a fine driver, but not much of a spieler. One fellow claimed a mountain was a better talker than the stringbean that drove behind the wheel of the bus — because you could at least get an echo back from a mountain.

"One pair of schoolteachers certainly got their money's worth, though. They came back all excited about the fascinating young fellow that drove them. This young fellow had told them about being born near Cody, but never getting into town until he was seventeen. When we asked them who the driver was, they pointed to Frank — leaning up against a post and chewing a straw. He never cracked a smile and looked as innocent as a prairie dog, though he'd gone to school in England and had managed to get around the country pretty well.

"He said the teachers roweled him till he had to tell 'em something. And when Frank decided to tell — he told."

So in his own quiet way, Coop was acting — although he never realized this until much later. He was acting when he was scaring the passengers half to death — because, as Boots said, "the rougher the ride the bigger the tip from the tourists, who'd be happy to come down alive." And Coop was also acting when he was giving the teachers a line.

Actually, Coop was not far now from the day when he would be acting for real — before the cameras of Hollywood.

CHAPTER FOUR

Headin' to Hollywood

As it does to all young men, the time had come for Frank Cooper to take stock of himself, to assess himself in terms of what he had done and what he wanted to do in the years ahead, to see where he had been and where he was going.

He had completed 3 years in Grinnell College and he was now 23 years old.

The year was 1924. The previous year, Justice Charles H. Cooper had resigned from the Montana Supreme Court and had returned to private law practice. But he did not forsake his own state Republican Party, which had elected him to the bench. He took an active leadership in its work. Coop, who decided not to return to college for his senior year, offered to help his dad by drawing political cartoons. The sketches were published in a number of Montana newspapers, much to the boy's delight. They were so well received that Coop's optimism zoomed and led him to think he could make good as a professional.

"I knew I could draw," Coop said years later, "but I

31

didn't know how well, and I wasn't absolutely confident that the style I had — or the ideas — were any good. I figured, at any rate, I'd need a little honing."

He decided to go to Chicago and enroll in art school.

One hurdle faced Coop. Money. He had saved about $350 from odd jobs he had performed at college, but that wasn't enough to see him through the professional art course he wanted to take. He was determined, however, and made up his mind to earn the money he'd need to see him through.

He could have asked his father for the money — and probably could have gotten it without trouble. Coop had lived now for 23 years of his life with his family, except for the time he was away at college. He had "lived high on the hog at home," as he himself used to put it after he became Gary Cooper, the movie star. But he also had fierce pride.

He was determined to earn the necessary money himself, even though he compromised somewhat by trying out the plans he had while living on his parents' generosity at home.

By the fall of 1924, Coop was a full-grown man in every respect. He was vigorous and reasonably well-educated. He had not set Grinnell College afire with his grades, but on the other hand a B average was nothing to sneeze at, and that was Cooper's achievement in his three years there.

Then something happened which drastically changed Coop's life.

His father and mother went to California.

It was a business trip. Charles Cooper had been engaged by a Montana client to untangle an estate case in Hollywood, and this required him to go to the Coast for a number of months. Coop's parents wanted him to come along, but he insisted on staying behind in Helena to seek the small bankroll for his art course in Chicago.

Months passed and Christmas approached. Coop received a letter from his dad.

"It appears I may be here on this case for a long time," wrote his father. "Mother and I both miss you. I think it would be a good thing if you ambled down this way and let mother see how her growing boy is doing. Besides, don't you miss her fine home cooking?"

The invitation was overpowering. Frank hadn't really eaten a good square meal since his mother and father left home. Actually, Coop's $350 bankroll had thinned perceptibly, since he hadn't been able to find any work in Helena.

Outside, snow was a foot deep. The winter was dead ahead.

What could he lose by going to Hollywood?

"I might starve," Coop once told Tex McCrary and Jinx Falkenburg during an interview, "but I figured at least I wouldn't freeze to death in Hollywood."

The trip was just what he needed. A nice warm climate, a comfortable bed to sleep in, and his mom's home cooking.

So he ambled down to the film capital.

There was more in the back of Coop's mind than the promise of a warm hearth, a good meal, and the happy reunion with his parents. Hollywood was right next door to Los Angeles, a big city with several large daily newspapers. With a little luck, he might land a job on one of them as a political cartoonist.

He arrived on the Coast within a week. A week later he had finished the rounds of all the newspapers. None of them, he found to his dismay, needed a cartoonist. Nor was there much likelihood of an opening in the foreseeable future. All the papers were staffed with bright young men just out of college or art school, and for every artist already working on the papers, a hundred others had applied and were on the waiting lists.

Determined to get some sort of drawing job, Frank temporarily abandoned political cartooning and found a job in a newspaper advertising department, drawing display ads. Describing this phase of his life in a biographical sketch prepared by Paramount Pictures, one of the many film companies with which he was under long-term contract, Coop said:

"It sounded great, the way the ad manager put it to me. All I'd have to do is whip up some kind of dazzlin' display and sweep the client off his feet with it. Pretty soon I'd have to fight the clients so that I'd have the necessary hours to count my commissions. It was a sure thing. Or so I was led to believe."

A few weeks later Frank quit. Something had gone wrong. The sales pitch he kept putting together simply didn't dazzle anyone.

"In those weeks I didn't make a single sale and didn't earn a red cent in commissions," Coop recalled.

A short time later, young Coop landed a job as a baby photographer. How and why could a man, determined to be an artist, ever find himself in a line of work so totally alien? Coop explained it years later to Mel Finkelstein, a photographer for the New York *Journal-American*. Finkelstein had been assigned to meet Coop on his arrival in New York after one of his numerous trips abroad. While the photographer was shooting, Coop asked about the Speed Graphic's strobe light attachment.

"Used to be a photographer once myself," Coop told Finkelstein. "Baby photographer. I had to take the job because there was nothing else around — but we never had anything as fancy as your camera."

Finkelstein recalled that Coop was quite voluble about the way he was roped into the deal.

"The guy who talked me into working for him should have been a carnival barker," Coop said. "What a salesman! Either that, or I was the most gullible kid in creation. He talked for about five minutes, telling me about the mother's love for her child and how no matter what else goes on in the world, that mother love never changes — and that it was a photographer's duty and privilege to give those mothers 'personal and intimate portraits' of their children; something lasting."

When Cooper finally did go out banging on doors to sell the portraits, he felt as if he were on some kind of mission. Perhaps the mothers themselves didn't know how precious their kids were, because when Coop tried to explain it in his sales pitch he'd get something like "Get lost, mister."

He kept at it for three or four weeks and didn't make a single sale.

"Needless to say," said Coop, "I quit."

Coop's next job during that peripatetic time was as a theatrical scene painter in a unique field. He apprenticed himself to a backdrop artist who had a penchant for only the brightest colors in the spectrum. The artist had achieved a fine reputation years before, painting on mirrors. His finest effort was on display in the Louvre — a saloon in North Los Angeles. But with the advent of Prohibition, the artist turned his talents to vaudeville and burlesque theater curtains.

Coop's assignment was to help the artist paint ads on the curtains — items like a lady's chapeau to advertise a hat store, or a plate of bacon and eggs to publicize a nearby hash house.

Happy to be back at art work — no matter how unusual the job might be — Coop threw himself into the endeavor.

But he'd hardly had a chance to swing a few strokes of yellow paint with his brush to create the yolk of an egg when — the artist and his business folded.

Out of work again and broke, Coop pondered his future. He decided to take a walk, to think things over. Coop had found one thing always helped when he was depressed — a walk.

"I discovered taking a walk always helped me dope out my problems," Coop often said. "I used to do a lot of walking when I was up on the ranch recovering from my injury in the auto accident. It enabled me to think clearly. It became a sort of habit the rest of my life."

On this particular day, Coop walked listlessly through the streets of Los Angeles for hours, knowing full well an important decision was at hand:

Should he stay on the West Coast and try once more for work?

Should he return to Montana?

How about art school?

"I figured," Coop said, "that I could always put the bite on dad as a last resort — but I was very reluctant, as I'd always been."

There was that fierce Cooper pride again.

Coop was pushing 24 and now the feeling that he had achieved nothing burdened him terribly.

What to do?

But now Coop had walked for miles, and without realizing it, his long knotty legs had finally taken him into another town, away from Los Angeles.

He was in Hollywood.

As he neared the intersection of Hollywood and Vine he was so deep in thought he scarcely noticed the two sorry-looking cowboys walking toward him. Even then he might have passed them by without a second thought except that one of them, fantastically, hollered, "Hi-ya, Frank!"

Coop squinted at the two cowboys. Their boots and clothes were caked with dirt, their shirts torn, their ten-gallon hats battered. Fresh red bruises were on their faces. Their eyes were half-closed with beautiful purplish-blue shiners. They looked as though they'd been run over by a herd of stampeding steers.

"Who the hell are these characters?" Coop thought. "How do these saddle-tramps know my name?"

He continued to stare at them, searching his memory for some clue to where he might have met them. Then the second cowboy yelled over: "What gives there, Frank — don't you recognize us? Has Hollywood made you too puffy-headed to give a couple of *pore* range rats from Montana a greetin'?"

Suddenly Coop's face lit up in a bright flash of recognition.

He grinned. How could he help but recognize them: Jimmy Galen, a boyhood chum from back home, and, of all people, Slim Talbot.

Accustomed as the sophisticated boulevardiers of Hollywood were to curious sights, they couldn't resist stopping to gawk at the odd trio shouting wild greetings back and forth.

"What in tarnation are you doin' down here?" Coop asked. "And what the hell happened to you? Why, it looks like you just rolled down a mountain."

"That's exactly what we've been doing," Talbot replied.

Coop looked bewildered.

"We're extras, in the movies," Talbot quickly explained.

"Extras!"

"Yeah — and the pay's great," Galen put in. "We get up to $25 a day."

"Then ... then ... you're actors? ... " Coop asked in astonishment.

Slim and Jimmy paled as if the word were obscene. They immediately chorused their protests at being called actors. They were Montanans, born and raised on the vast open ranges of the real West. Riding and handling horses were as natural to them as getting up in the morning. A cowboy, to them, was a real person, an integral part of their boyhood landscape, a usually tough, often lonely, always broke, gritty character in loose-fitting leather chaps, dirty shirt, cracked boots. He drank hard and lived hard and generally moved on when the wandering spirit stirred within him. He was the true, genuine cowboy; and when a Montanan saw the prissy, sissified Hollywood version on the screen, the counterfeit with the guitar and the always-immaculate, silver-spangled white steed beneath him, he'd fall into convulsions of laughter — if he didn't get nauseous first.

Well, if they weren't actors, what were they, Coop asked. How come they were doing this Wild West "extra" stuff in front of *cameras?*

"Well, Frank, we work in the movies," Talbot offered. "We do that, all right. But we're not actors. We're extras — that's different than being an actor. They hire us because we show those city-slicker actor guys how to ride and how to fall off horses. They're too soft to do that. And we get good money for it."

As Talbot talked, Coop began to visualize himself as an extra. He certainly needed the money, and the way his friends described it, being an extra seemed easy enough.

"D'ya think I could get a job like that?" Coop asked.

"Sure ya can," Galen told him. "Lots of jobs for good ridin' cowboys like you over at Fox. Course, you may not get 25 bucks right away. Maybe they'll start you off at five, or even ten. But if you show 'em what you can do in the saddle, and off of it, you'll get up there in the high-payin' brackets."

"Come on," Talbot said, "we'll find you work."

Slim and Jimmy took Frank Cooper down to Poverty Row, a ramshackle stretch of old Hollywood where the makers of quickie Western films maintained headquarters in those days of silent pictures.

They introduced him to a casting director who was lining up players for a picture about the Boer War. The director was looking for bold, devil-may-care riders to take part in a sequence of daring cavalry maneuvers. When he saw Coop, he let his eyes gaze over the tall, angular figure.

"Greatest rider to come out of Montana," said Talbot.

"Don't come any better," offered Galen.

"Looks like a dude to me," countered the director.

Talbot and Galen protested that just because Coop was dressed in a suit it didn't mean he couldn't ride a horse.

"Yeah," the director shot back, "but can he fall off a mount? Eh, how about it, kid?" The director was glaring at Coop.

Coop swallowed hard.

"Do it all the time," he said, straightfaced.

"Okay, kid, you're hired . . . go over to wardrobe and tell them to give you a beard and a uniform."

Cooper was stunned, but not any more than were Galen and Talbot. Coop's immediate concern was for his friends. He wanted to know whether he was doing them out of work by being taken on.

"Don't be silly," Slim said, "there's plenty of work around for all of us. This is your big chance. The more of us Montanans who get in the movies the better it is for us to get jobs. As for what I think you are, I'll tell ya.

"You're an actor now!"

There's a touch of irony in this story, irony typical of Hollywood, of the topsy-turvy kind of world it is. Success is for some, failure for others. Achievement, oblivion — Fate deals her cards swiftly in the glittering capital of the cinema world.

Of the three young men who had stormed the citadels of moviedom in 1925, one was destined to go back home to a Montana ranch — Jimmy Galen. The second might have become famous, except for one fault, unpardonable in the movies — he resembled a star. This young man was Jay "Slim" Talbot.

And the star was his pal, Gary Cooper, who succeeded and captured elusive fame, fortune, and screen immortality.

But Slim's future was still in Hollywood, although obscure in contrast with Coop's. Slim Talbot was to become Gary Cooper's stand-in.

CHAPTER FIVE

Camera! Action! Fall!

Frank Cooper's first movie job was as a cavalry rider in a fast-moving epic about the Boer War, and even those who later credited him with attaining the most subtle gradations of thespian skill would not quarrel with the observation that his debut labeled him as an inordinately luckless fall guy — a patsy to a horse.

When he showed up on the movie lot after the director hired him, Coop was one of forty cowboy extras in a scene portraying not the Wild West but the British Cavalry in deadly combat with the South Africans at the turn of the century.

Their location was an overworked patch of Western "prairie," a forgotten monument of those pioneering days of filmland that now lies under the sprawling community of Burbank. On that December morning in 1924, the locale provided the ideal authenticity of any outdoor setting a director wished to duplicate. Much of the time it served as a prairie; other times it was a battlefield — as for this scene, Coop's first in movies.

41

It all started this way, Coop related:

"I put on my phony black beard and a uniform and went with the other extras to a big bus on the Fox lot. We were driven up to the mountains to do our bit for Britain."

Coop and the others waited for the director to show up. He arrived breathless and anxious to roll the cameras — perhaps not so much that he was dedicated to his art and itched to begin creating as that 1924 was the era of mass-produced one- and two-reelers, and any director who couldn't finish his shooting schedule in nine or ten days was considered something of a nitwit and an extravagant wastrel.

This was the heyday of the quickie Western. They were being cranked out almost faster than Henry Ford was turning out Model Ts.

With the director came his subordinates — the assistant directors, the associate directors, the unit directors. It was one of the unit directors who took immediate command of the cowboy extras.

"The director told us what the scene was all about," Coop recalled. "Then he ordered us to get on our mounts and to wait for his signal, which was a blank gun that he would fire when ready. Each of us was given a rifle. The director came up to me and said, 'You, there. When this charge gets under way, I want you to ride along with the bunch halfway down this field. Then throw your rifle in the air and fall off your horse. Got it?'

"I nodded my head that I understood. I understood, all right — but I wasn't quite sure how I'd manage the fall. I'd never tried falling off a horse before."

Then the gun went off. The charge was on.

"In the middle of the dash across this field, I threw my rifle into the air just like the director told me to do and slid off my horse. I hit the ground with a shuddering jolt. I went head over heels — then lay very quiet, playing dead as a mackerel."

Then the director rushed up.

"Great ... you were simply great!" he shouted. "Now I want you to do it again."

And then there was another fall.

Did Coop mind? Well, not really.

"Guess the thing that really made me do it so willingly was the *extra* pay for falling off a horse — five dollars a fall. At the end of the first day, I was paid fifteen dollars extra, twenty dollars all told. 'Course I had a bruise for each dollar of it — but that one day's work kind of convinced me that movies might make a living for a fellow if he would only stick to it."

Coop had his first lesson in moviemaking, and he was quite ready to grant that acting, as he was introduced to it, was not a sissy occupation.

The days flew by and with each one, Coop found himself suffering, yet enjoying this new work more and more. It may have been rough and sometimes bone-crushing, but it was clean, and it was fun, and there was attached to it all the glamor of the movies. Ruefully at first, but then with less and less self-consciousness, Coop admitted to himself that he was, indeed, a movie actor, no matter how insignificant at the moment, and that he actually liked the idea.

There were other rewards. The five dollars a fall, the camaraderie of working with other bona fide horsemen, and — a little bonus the studios threw in on location — free lunch in the commissary tent, usually a plate of spicy stew and a canteen of coffee.

Now and then, when he'd take an especially painful fall or if he wasn't satisfied with the way he was doing his work, Coop would shake his head, turn his thoughts inward, and tell himself to "Quit now while the quittin's good."

But the joys more than compensated for his troubles, and Coop stayed with it determinedly. One main reason was the encouragement he got from home. Coop's parents learned about their son's exploits on the movie lots on the very first day. How could they help not noticing the bruises on his face, the way he hunched his shoulders cautiously and moved with a slow deliberation that told them he was in pain? There must be some explanation. It came after Frank washed up and joined his mother and father at the dinner table.

"What happened to you, Frank?" asked Mr. Cooper. "Have an argument with a truck?"

"No, sir," replied young Cooper, his mind made up to handle everything straightforwardly no matter how disdainful his folks might be of actors and acting. "I'm an actor — a cowboy extra in the movies. But it's quite respectable and there's plenty of money in it. Not right now, maybe, but there will be later on. Now I'm making five dollars every time I fall off a horse . . . I made twenty bucks today, yes, sirree."

Frank looked down at the table and busied himself with the food on his plate. He tried to steady his trembling hands; afraid to look up, afraid to look his parents in the face. He was reasonably certain he had caused them to be horrified. The intense silence that followed strengthened that conviction until he heard his father's voice.

"Son," it started out, "you're a man now. You know what you want out of life. Anything you decide is all right with me, but then you'd go right ahead and do it anyway, and if you didn't, you wouldn't be my son. . . ."

Frank lifted his eyes and gazed across the table at his father as he spoke, then slowly he glanced over at his mother. Her face was an inscrutable mask. He continued to listen to his father's advice, but kept his eyes on his mother. Inside he felt a warm encouragement as his father said, "Go after it, Frank, and put everything you've got into it. . . . Shoot for the top. If you get close, you've done all right in your lifetime. . . ."

Still Frank Cooper searched his mother's face, hoping she'd reflect some of his father's sentiments.

"Mom," he finally said, almost interrupting his father, "I'm doing the right thing, believe me. . . . Dad just said so, didn't he?"

At long last Mrs. Cooper allowed herself to smile.

"Yes, Frank, I'm sure you are doing right. I'm with you all the way. Only, tell me this, Frank — will you always look the way you do now?"

Young Cooper had forgotten for the moment that his face was a mass of bruises.

The meal ended on a fine burst of laughter. ˷

Reinforced by the knowledge his parents supported his decision, and aware that he had committed himself to his new career, Coop plunged ahead with renewed vigor. In a short time he became the acknowledged virtuoso of the "fall-down" boys and was constantly sought for what the directors, for some reason, called their "showcase falls" — usually a hell-for-leather, dust-kicking tumble a scant dozen feet from the camera that would sum up, in one breath-sucking bit of action, the ferocity of the battle then raging on the screen.

Each day Frank Cooper would hobble off the set, bruised and battered, only to return the following day for more of the same punishment. But in the process, he realized, he was achieving a unique place in the annals of Hollywood. Cast as a one-man massacre, Coop's fame as a horse-faller-offer spread so widely that hardly a day passed when he wasn't hired for his special brand of equine acrobatics.

He had hit paydirt by hitting the real dirt.

In those days, the cameras turned relentlessly. Shooting schedules then ran about ten days at the most. If the pictures were epics, as the big ones were called in those days, they might take up to two or three weeks.

But work for the extras never remotely approached the full shooting schedule. Economy was the rule by which every reel of film was shot. Thus every shortcut, every penny-pinching device was used that could be put in practice effectively. A cowboy extra like Coop worked a full day on location, falling off his steed, chasing a stagecoach, or doing the hundreds of other action-filled scenes that the directors demanded of him.

The extra would then wait a few weeks to see the film in which he played in one of the Hollywood movie houses. He'd be amazed to see that only a portion of his hard work was exhibited on the screen. What happened to the other exciting scenes? A week or a month, or even a year later, he might get the answer if he went to the movies regularly. He could see himself in perhaps a half-dozen other Westerns in which he had never worked a day. This was all done in the cutting rooms — utilizing one man's or a group of actors' single day's efforts in an endless number of films.

Nevertheless, the extras were content to work that way, especially Frank Cooper, whose salary had in a short time gone up from five dollars a fall to ten. Like all the other extras, Coop was spliced by ingenious moviemakers into many more films than he could ever know he had played in.

"I'll bet there were a couple of hundred quickie Westerns that had me doing something or other in the action which I never had wind I was a part of," Coop said. "I guess I was like all the other guys in those days — happy to make a buck. We didn't seem to care how much advantage the studios took of us, so long as they paid us."

The weeks went into months and Coop toiled untiringly in picture after picture. Six months had swiftly gone by and Coop suddenly came to a realization — he had reached his peak in doing spectacular flying falls off a stallion's back. Coop wondered now whether every next fall might not be his last.

Actually, Coop had gotten an occasional crack at some bit acting. He had held a horse for Billie Dove, helped to shoe Dustin Farnum's steed, caught Tom Mix in a scene when the $17,500-a-week cowboy star was shot off a horse, played an Indian with Richard Dix, and a Cossack with Rudolph Valentino.

Yet, while he got his small share of bit parts, the great bulk of his work, day in and day out, was slugging some varmint during a saloon donnybrook or falling off a horse, and he was becoming increasingly apprehensive about his future.

He realized, for one thing, that he couldn't go on indefinitely in such physically punishing work. For another, he could see where the big money lay in Hollywood. If he were going to remain in the movies, he reasoned, he might as well shoot for the big jackpot.

"What really convinced me," Cooper said later, "was the salary Tom Mix was getting. He was pulling down $17,500 a week. I was flabbergasted. Imagine, $17,500 a week in those days. It convinced me there was a good deal more money in the movie business than the few bucks I was drawing."

Cooper had an idea that there was money to be made in Hollywood long before he descended upon the movie citadel. It was brought to his attention back home in Montana when he was a teenager. The seed was planted by a lawyer — not his dad but a man named Wellington Rankin, brother of Jeanette Rankin, first woman elected to the

U. S. House of Representatives. The anecdote was told by Coop in a reminiscence of his early life for *McCall's* magazine shortly before his death.

Coop and Rankin were discussing Rudolph Valentino, who was the nation's movie idol. Even in Montana, when the kids saw the effect Valentino had on the girls, they quickly adopted him as their movie hero. William S. Hart and Tom Mix were no match, because the kids wanted to emulate not those heroes of the Wild West, but Valentino — the lover. So much so that they dressed like Valentino, smiled like Valentino, and even plastered their hair down with shiny "greasy kid stuff" like Valentino. Not just in Montana, but everywhere in the United States and in other countries, too. But in Montana, as perhaps in few other states, the kids' appearance after doing themselves up like the "Great Lover" of the screen hardly blended with the cowboy country that Helena was then. But that's the way Valentino hit people everywhere. Everyone tried to imitate him.

So it was that day when lawyer Rankin talked about Valentino.

Coop quoted Rankin as saying to him:

"Look how this fellow puts over an idea. He thinks of what he is doing. He thinks of it so strongly that it becomes obvious to the audience. When he looks at a girl, you know he's thinking of taking the clothes off her. You know that when he walks up and kisses her, he is sort of halfway beyond the kiss already."

Coop claimed that Rankin's insight served to take him out of his dilemma in his later years in Hollywood when directors confused Gary with their incessant and interminable demands and instructions.

But in those early days in Montana, Coop could not have imagined himself as a Valentino, nor as anyone who could wield such terrific power over women. As yet he hadn't even begun to go with girls. That didn't come until later, when he went to Grinnell College — and when he worked in Yellowstone, where his contacts with many young lady tourists led him to take some of them out on dates.

Coop never credited Rankin with being the person who planted the seed in his mind about becoming an actor. But possibly he was. Actually, Coop's first real interest in acting was at Grinnell, where he tried out for the dramatic club but flopped.

"Grinnell wasn't about to give me my start on the stage," Coop said years later.

Nor, it seemed, was Hollywood too anxious to catapult Frank Cooper into great prominence as an actor in his first year on the scene. The film capital had plenty of need for Coop as a "fall guy" on a horse — but no starring roles. He wasn't about to push Valentino into limbo.

It was this realization that suddenly brought Cooper to the verge of uncertainty about his future in Hollywood. He decided to give himself a little more time, perhaps five or six months more. After that, if he had not progressed beyond the anonymous status of a cowboy extra, he'd quit the movies and head East for Chicago to pursue his artistic yearnings.

Frank had a talk with his father about his plan.

"Strikes me, son, that I know someone who might help you," Mr. Cooper told Frank. That someone was Mrs. J. Charles Davis, but in those infant days of the movies she was known as Marilyn Mills — an actress, a star at that, and a producer of movies.

Miss Mills had been looking for someone to play a supporting role in a new film called *Tricks*. She already had her costar, J. Frank Glendon, who would be the hero of the horse opera.

It was an awesome moment for Cooper when he came

face to face with Marilyn Mills. He was overwhelmed by her importance. Suddenly he found himself stammering.

"I'm v-v-very anxious t-to w-w-work in a f-f-featured r-r-role," Cooper managed to blurt out after the introductions. He was perspiring.

"Your dad says you want to play the heavy," Miss Mills smiled politely, eyeing the lanky and shy young man who towered over her, uncomfortably and nervously, shifting his weight from one foot to the other, uncertain of what to do with his hands, which were useless and in the way. "Is that what you want?" Miss Mills asked.

Cooper struggled to find his tongue. He broke into a small, shy grin.

"Y-y-yes, m-m-ma'am," he finally replied.

Marilyn Mills saw something in Cooper's manner that she liked. She decided then and there that he was going to play the villain in *Tricks*.

He was probably one of the tallest, thinnest extras who ever sat in a saddle — and certainly, now, he was about to become one of the tallest, thinnest villains in film history. Everything about Coop was thin — his wrists, his arms, his legs, his waist, his chest.

"Any way you looked at me," Coop recalled, "I was a mass of sharp edges and points."

This was the picture Cooper saw of himself when he had reached the crossroads of his life, back in 1925. This was the day Coop had to report on the set to begin shooting. Miss Mills's recollection of the incident, related by Jack Hirshberg, of the Rogers & Cowan agency which handled Cooper, was amusing.

"That morning at the appointed hour when we were to shoot *Tricks*, there he was on my doorstep. I never saw so much humanity in one piece. We drove out to location and when director Bruce Mitchell saw this stringbean crawl out of the car he blew his top. He said he'd have to dig a hole and put Cooper in it or he'd make all the other actors look like midgets. He said he would never let Cooper in a scene with our leading man, Frank Glendon, unless Glendon was on a horse and Coop remained in the background."

When director Mitchell sounded off so blatantly, Coop began to feel himself coming to a slow boil, but it never showed; he suddenly found he was no longer awed by Miss Mills or Glendon or Mitchell. Coop was downright sore. Inside.

Then in a voice as gentle as ever, almost as soft as a caress, he replied to the man who had belittled him:

"You may not be aware of it, but I don't pretend that my acting ability is of the highest quality. Nor do I pretend to hide my physical faults — if they are faults. But I have been imbued with enough of the spirit of acting to bring quality into anything I do and to benefit those for whom I perform."

Mitchell was taken aback by the courteous challenge. He stared at Coop blankly.

The uneasy silence was broken by Miss Mills who said: "He'll work out. . . . I'm sure of that."

From that moment on, Miss Mills took a personal interest in the lanky, awkward, bashful cowboy. One day not long afterward she came to him with this advice:

"Coop, if you're ever going to get anywhere in this business, you'll have to put some meat on that skinny frame of yours. Try eating bananas — with breakfast, lunch, and dinner. Eat bananas all the time."

Coop, who had weighed 175 pounds when he came to Hollywood, had dropped to 155 during his first several months of grueling work as an extra, falling off horses and stagecoaches. But after following Miss Mills's suggestion to eat bananas, he quickly ran his weight up to 170.

Coop made it through *Tricks* in grand style as a heavy. So well did he perform that Miss Mills immediately put him in a second film, *Three Pals*, another Western.

But when that picture was finished, Coop felt that playing the villain was all right to gain acting experience; but he had no ambition to make a career of it.

"I had no real formal training in dramatics," Coop explained later. "I had watched, perhaps with awe, how some of my counterparts of those days exaggerated in their acting. My own method, I told myself, was far less complicated — I simply felt that I wanted to be myself in any part I played. I wanted to be able to imagine how I'd feel and behave in a given set of circumstances, and act accordingly."

Since Coop was a guy who had grown up on the side of law and order, since he was a guy who believed in "naturalness," and since he was a guy who had made up his mind to get what he went after — Coop quit the Mills–Glendon film combine. He went looking for other work — as a hero.

But hero roles weren't lining the streets of Hollywood, not even in those days.

And no one was more aware of the fact than Coop, who — unable to find work anywhere — inevitably wound up on the street.

It is interesting to note that the records of those early years, as compiled by Coop's agents, who should know his film roles, show he played the part of the villain twice — in *Tricks* and *Three Pals*. Yet years later, Coop sometimes looked back on those hectic times with vague recollections.

"I only played the villain once," Coop told Hal Boyle, the distinguished Associated Press columnist, on December 11, 1954. "It was in a two-reel quickie made on Pov-

erty Row. I played the heavy who set fire to the widow —
or was it her mortgage?"

Whether it was once as he had claimed or twice as the
record shows, the fact remains that Gary Cooper became
one of the truly all-time greats of moviedom — a hero to
the very last.

But in 1925, Coop was no more a hero to himself than
to the various studios around town which wouldn't give
him a tumble.

He was just another out-of-work actor.

A Poetic Change—
Gary Cooper

▌▐▐▐▐█▐██▐▌▐█▐██▌▐█▐██▐▌▐█▐██▌▐█▐██▐▌▐█▐██▌▐█▐▌█

Frank Cooper could have gone back to Poverty Row, or Gower's Gulch, as that dumpy moviemaking sector of Hollywood was known in that era. He could have returned to falling out of saddles. But he didn't want that again. He wanted to act. However, there was one hitch — not only wouldn't the studios give Coop a break — they even turned him down when he asked for a screen test.

In a rare departure from the normal ego-inflating brand of self-analysis, Frank Cooper studied himself honestly and recognized his shortcomings for what they were. He decided to do something about them — by himself if he could but with the help of others if necessary.

He realized he was one of the tallest, scrawniest, angular actors who ever appeared on horseback — or off. He looked like "a long drink of water."

Despite trick camera techniques that Miss Mills had used — shooting half or three-quarter length of Cooper instead of his entire height — Frank was still not com-

54

pletely satisfied that good camera work was all that was needed to eliminate his awkward appearance. He considered enrolling in drama classes, but chucked the idea after some deliberation. He stuck by his idea that he was going to bring "naturalness" to the screen; and the way he would do that was by being himself. Lessons couldn't improve him. Something else would have to be done to put Frank Cooper's movie career in high gear.

He decided to consult with a Hollywood agent named Nan Collins.

Miss Collins looked at the towering young man standing in front of her desk and studied him in silence. Then she got up and stepped back to get the full view of him. She let her scrutinizing gaze roam for several seconds over Coop's big frame, taking in the long neck, the arms, the legs, the knees, the elbows, and then, after a pause, she said:

"I'm going to get Marilyn Mills to put together some scenes of you in *Tricks* and *Three Pals* and send them to Sam Goldwyn," Miss Collins promised. "But I can see that there isn't going to be much of a problem with your acting. I think you'll make it — except there's one thing wrong."

"What's that?" Coop asked.

"We've got to change your name."

"Do what?"

"Change your name. Don't be disturbed. It's done all the time out here."

Coop was horrified.

"No, sir . . . I mean, no, ma'am. Not that. No monkeyin' around with my name. I won't stand for it."

"Wait a minute now, Mr. Cooper," Miss Collins put in hastily. "I'm not suggesting we change your last name. As a matter of fact, I rather like it. Has a nice ring. Cooper. Yes, very nice. What I mean is that Frank doesn't seem to go with it. And there are some other Frank Coopers in the movies. I know of at least one other."

"What do you mean, 'doesn't go with it'? " Coop asked, ignoring the fact that there were other Frank Coopers in Hollywood. "I was born Frank Cooper and I've been Frank Cooper since." Cooper was still ruffled. "Of course they go together."

"Well," said Miss Collins, "it doesn't excite me . . ."

"It excites me," Cooper said firmly.

That was how the first meeting between Coop and Miss Collins ended. Frank Cooper let some time pass before he went back to Miss Collins. Meanwhile, he had found no employment since his last bit for Marilyn Mills in *Three Pals*. He was broke; Coop had spent every cent he'd made. He had bought fancy clothes, had gone nightclubbing, and had done the town up red.

Aside from needing a job desperately, Coop had become acutely aware of something.

"Every time I looked at a newspaper," he recalled later, "some guy named Frank Cooper was getting in trouble. I knew they couldn't be kin of mine, not all those counterfeiters, embezzlers, burglars, wife-deserters — the whole gamut — all named Frank Cooper. I think the last straw and the thing that made me change my mind was when I read that a Frank Cooper in Chicago was on trial for killing his wife. It was a big, sensational story at that time. I thought about it a while and then called on Miss Collins."

"Okay, Nan, you win," Cooper said. "You got any particular name in mind?"

"I do," Miss Collins said. "I've been thinking about it — just in case you changed your mind. I'm from Indiana. My home town was named after Elbert H. Gary. I think Gary has a nice poetic sound to it. I'd like to see you take Elbert Gary's last name for your first."

"You mean," he interrupted, "Gary Cooper?"

"Yes — Gary Cooper. Say it again. Gary Cooper. Very nice. I like it. Don't you?"

Gary Cooper.

He ran the name around in his mind a few times. He spoke it again.

Gary Cooper.

Then he smiled. "I like it."

"You see," Miss Collins said. "I knew you would. And you'll have to agree, Gary Cooper doesn't sound as tall and lanky as Frank Cooper."

Coop couldn't quite catch Nan's logic in that; nevertheless he was satisfied. All at once he grimaced.

"What's the matter, Fr . . . I mean, Gary?"

"I just had a horrible thought," he told Miss Collins. "Suppose you had come from Poughkeepsie?"

Miss Collins failed to work any immediate miracles. Sam Goldwyn wasn't particularly impressed with the film clips of Gary's efforts for Marilyn Mills which the agent had sent over for a screening. However, Miss Collins managed to get Cooper small parts in a number of important films. But they were very small parts. She also managed to swing one lead his way. It was just a quickie Western made on Poverty Row, called *Lightning Justice*, directed by Al Nietz.

In his study of Coop's early years, Jack Hirshberg said this was the first time that Coop's name appeared in the titles. And it appeared not as Frank Cooper — but Gary Cooper.

Soon afterward Gary Cooper was cast in another starring role, playing in a two-reel Western opposite Eileen Sedgewick and a police dog of some note.

"Gary shared honors with Rin-Tin-Tin," is how Hollywood columnist Louella Parsons put it in describing Coop's efforts in this opus.

Cooper wasn't altogether pleased with these accomplishments. The income from two-reelers was not much better than the money he had been making as an extra, and in the latter case he could sometimes fall from a horse often enough to pile up twenty or even thirty dollars a day. As a "star" in his first Westerns, Coop barely pulled down fifty a week. It was a dismal situation. How could he keep up with the payments on his fancy red roadster, which he had bought to drive around the film capital as an up-and-coming man-about-town?

Coop decided that he would have to take matters into his own hands. His first move was to make a direct assault on the studios himself, actually covering ground already gone over by Miss Collins in her efforts to latch on to a contract for her client.

At Goldwyn, the answer was no.

At Fox, the answer was no.

At Warner's, the answer was no.

At Paramount, the answer was no.

Get the idea?

Coop did and by now he was ready to call it quits. And he would have quit, if he hadn't come up with one of the shrewdest ideas ever to be hatched in the movie capital, where shrewd ideas are abundant.

Coop had about $65 to his name.

"If no one will give me a screen test," he asked himself, "why not produce my own?"

Yup, a great idea, he thought.

Coop would make his own screen test. . . .

CHAPTER SEVEN

A Do-It-Yourself Screen Test

"You want to do what?"

"I want to make a screen test and I've come to you to do it for me. Don't worry — I'm gonna pay for your services."

"Let me get this straight, friend. You want me to shoot a screen test that you're going to produce, direct, act in — and pay for?"

"That's the way it's gonna be. Now, all you gotta do is tell me what you're chargin' me. And you'd better go easy because I haven't got much money."

A fast exchange of words — puzzled questions from the beret-clad photographer and patient answers from the tall, rawboned visitor — made it clear that Gary Cooper was determined to make his own screen test.

The photographer studied Coop long and penetratingly. He found it hard to conceal the expression of curiosity, bewilderment, even annoyance that washed across his face in alternate waves. He was one of the many slaves of the movie camera toiling for the companies along Poverty Row; he had filmed many of the pictures in which Gary Cooper had appeared as a cowboy extra.

Coop waited anxiously for the photographer to name his price, hoping it would be within the scope of the $65 pocketed in his trousers.

"You're going to use a horse in this test?"

Coop's idea had generated an odd, gnawing curiosity in the photographer. He seemed to rejoice in the prospect of the assignment, which suddenly held precious possibilities, all of them studded thick with mercenary thoughts.

"How much you got?" the photographer inquired, without any sense of shame or inclination to strike a bargain in more subtle ways.

Coop frowned, tightened his lips, put his hand into his pocket.

"Sixty-five dollars," he said blandly, depositing the money in the photographer's open, outstretched hand.

"I'll have to get you a horse," the photographer muttered as he counted the money. "I'm not going to make anything on this deal, but I'll do it as a favor."

Coop smiled wanly. He was thinking, "You chiseler."

The production was simple and swift. The small budget did not allow elaborate preparations and exquisite settings. The location was on the idle set of a small Western main street, located just off Poverty Row.

"Ready to roll!" the photographer shouted as Coop got astride his borrowed mount.

"Action!"

"Camera!"

Coop sunk his spurs into the horse and charged the camera.

Never in all his years as one of Hollywood's most durable actors did Coop forget this scene — to him personally an achievement worthy of an Academy Award.

"I was a venture capitalist," Cooper told Jinx Falkenburg and Tex McCrary in their "New York Close-Up"
column in the New York *Herald Tribune.*

"Sound pictures were still three years away when I
financed my own screen test. I scraped together every plug
nickel to my name — 65 bucks."

He went on to describe how he hired the camera man
"who didn't seem to mind taking my money. . . ."

Then Coop told Tex and Jinx how his ride went during
that fateful do-it-yourself screen test:

"I rode my horse wide open, then pulled up fast and
made a running dismount — next, I took off my hat, turned
my head so they could see all sides — and then I smiled
and looked happy . . . or something.

"I didn't know what I was doing!"

Coop knew just what to do with the film when the photographer had processed it.

He took it around to the studios. But getting them to run
it off was something of a problem. Even in those early
years, film companies were accustomed to picking their
own candidates for screen tests and running their own
cameras on the subject in situations they decided were best
suited for the actor.

According to Ezra Goodman, writing in the New York
Times, Coop's screen test did not get any immediate reception. But when he finally got someone to look at it, it was
a sort of turning point in his life.

"After eleven months," Coop told Goodman, "I got a
call from Sam Goldwyn. The part called for riding a horse.
That was my first real part — in *The Winning of Barbara
Worth.*"

But during those eleven months he hunted for someone
to look at his screen test, Coop also tried different ap-

proaches at the studios. One was sending out a collection of glossy prints of himself in an assortment of poses — including several in which he tried to look like Rudolph Valentino, hair slicked down, eyes half-drooping, and trying desperately to be the image of the Great Lover. The pictures were taken by his former employer — the baby photographer. The directors, however, were not impressed with either the picture collection or Coop.

In the meantime, he made the acquaintance of a studio makeup man who taught Coop the finer points of preparing his face for the camera. He showed Gary how to apply eye shadow and paint a cupid's bow on his lips. Coop worked on the techniques at home when he wasn't out banging on studio doors for work. And he also got himself a new agent.

But it wasn't the agent but Coop who had the drive to seek employment before the cameras.

His break finally came when he went to the Goldwyn Studios again and asked to see Henry King, who even then was a movie director of note. King was tied up with Sam Goldwyn in conference. Henry was to direct *The Winning of Barbara Worth* and was talking the picture over with the boss.

Coop was waiting in the office when King returned, and the director couldn't help noticing the tall young man seated in a straight-backed chair, hunched over with his arms wound around his legs.

According to Pete Martin, writing on this episode in the *Saturday Evening Post*, King asked his assistant director who the stranger was.

"Name's Cooper," the assistant replied. "Says he'd give his left arm to talk to you."

King walked over to the lean visitor and said, "OK, let's talk."

Coop was so nervous he barely could speak. He had

come prepared to sell himself to the director, yet now in King's presence Coop was overawed.

"He was so nervous I had to pull the words out of him," King said years later when he recalled that meeting for Martin.

Coop, who had heard that a certain part was open in the movie, stammered:

"I-I-I've c-c-come to t-t-try out for the L-L-Lee part in your m-m-movie. . . ."

He was referring to the role of Abe Lee, the second male lead. Ronald Colman already had been signed to play the lead and his costar was Vilma Banky, who had been publicized as the most beautiful woman in the world to the rapidly growing legion of movie followers all over the country.

King was taken aback by the newcomer's presumptuousness. He was momentarily without an answer — although the reply would have to be no. King had already picked someone for Lee's part — Harold "Al" Goodwin, a big name in films. At the moment Goodwin was tied up at Warner, on another film. But King expected Harold to be ready when shooting on *The Winning of Barbara Worth* got under way.

"Sorry," King said finally, "but the part is already assigned."

Then the director caught sight of a flat, round can in Cooper's lap.

"What's that?" he asked.

Coop stood up and thrust the can at King.

"It's my screen test," Gary said softly as if it were expected of every actor who tried for a part to carry his own can of film with him.

King looked at Coop with amazement.

"What studio made your test?" King asked.

"Didn't have it made at any studio," Coop replied. "Made it myself."

King shook his head. He was bewildered. Truly bewildered. He had never heard of an actor who made his own screen test.

"Let's take it into the projection room and run it through," he said, his curiosity greatly aroused.

It took less than a minute to run off the test. There was Coop on his rented mount, charging toward the screen; then as he pulled his horse to a braking stop in front of a rail fence, Coop leaped from the mount, ducked under the fence, doffed his hat, smiled, and it was all over.

The projection room lights went on and Coop, barely able to contain his anxiety, sat dead still in his chair staring at the screen, waiting for King to say the first word.

King was enthusiastic. "I like the way you ride — you're a good horseman. Where did you learn to handle a mount like that?"

"On my dad's ranch in Montana," Gary replied.

"I think we can use you," King said. "I've got a part in mind for you. Had another actor lined up, but I'd like to try you out for it."

Coop all but shouted with delight.

King ordered Gary to report to the casting director.

That afternoon, Coop was called before the camera to try out for the part. He was to play a messenger and pretend he had just completed a fifty-mile dash across arid countryside finally to reach a water hole, dying of thirst. He was supposed to lean over and drink from the water hole.

Coop's performance was hardly the way an actor with any training and experience would have done it.

"Gary simply blew the dust from the water," King related, "and dippered the water with his hands to his mouth. It wasn't polished acting — but it was real, just as he had learned to do it on the range up in Montana. I liked that. Coop had that elusive quality — naturalness."

King decided to hire him.

"I'm going to let you ride for me and do bit parts," the director told Coop. "I'll pay you fifty dollars a week and expenses. How does that suit you?"

"J-j-just s-s-swell . . . ," Coop stammered.

Coop approached his new picture with fear, but also with an eager desire to make the grade. While his part as a messenger in the film gave promise of less exposure before the camera than he received in Miss Mills's two productions as the heavy, nevertheless he was thrilled by the prospect of appearing in a Sam Goldwyn movie with its roster of great stars.

As shooting got under way on location, Goodwin was unable to show up immediately for work because he was still working on his picture at Warner Brothers. The shooting schedule on *The Winning of Barbara Worth* suddenly was confronted with the prospect of expensive time-consuming delays.

"Coop," said King one day when he reached the end of his patience waiting for Goodwin. "How'd you like to double for Al? I'll put you into his clothes and use you on the long shots. At a distance no one will know the difference."

"I'm game," Gary replied, delighted with the idea, of course.

When the long shots were done, interior closeups came up on the shooting schedule. The company had now returned to Hollywood. But Al Goodwin was still at Warner.

King approached Coop on the set early on the morning of the first day back. He eyed the lanky giant who already had played most of Abe Lee's role by performing in all the outdoor scenes. The director regarded Coop with a pleasurable gaze, rubbed his hands gleefully, and said, "Coop, you'll do."

"I'll do what?" Gary asked, puzzled.

"You'll do for the closeups — in fact you're going to end up playing Abe Lee."

Coop was exhilarated by the opportunity. It meant he could play the "other man" in love with Vilma Banky.

The part called for Lee to arrive bone-weary after a twenty-four-hour trek across a dry Western prairie, drag himself up the stairs of a frontier hotel, knock on a door, and collapse as it was opened — and he would collapse in the arms of none other than the star of the film, Ronald Colman.

"What a break for me," Coop would say years later. He always regarded this as his first real opportunity in movies. But if Coop had to do it over, he said, he might have been reluctant to go through again what he had to do then.

"We've got to make you look tired and beat," King said.

The director called makeup men and ordered them to wet Coop's face. Then they powdered him with fuller's earth — an absorbent clay — to give him the appearance of a dirt-caked dispatch rider returning from an arduous journey.

While the makeup men worked on Gary, the director tried to work up a feeling of exhaustion in his substitute Abe Lee.

"You've got to look like you're on your last legs when you walk into the hotel," King kept repeating. "You've never had it so rough . . . it's the toughest ride you ever went on. . . ."

Coop listened intently to the director. But he wasn't that all-fired tired. And he didn't think he could ever be. King somehow sensed that, and when the makeup men had finished caking Coop's face with "prairie dust," the director summoned the actor to one side of the set.

"Start walking!" King said.

"Where to?" Coop inquired.

"To the end of the stage and back. And when you return, I want you to do it again — and again until I tell you to stop."

Obediently Coop followed King's instructions. Back and forth he went — five times, ten, fifteen, fifty. . . .

It was noon. Coop had been walking three hours straight. By now his walk had slowed to a shuffle.

"You look great!" King shouted.

"Maybe to you I do," Coop said, "but I'm bushed."

"Let's run through the scene," ordered King.

"Lights! Camera! Roll 'em!"

And Coop dragged himself into the hotel, ascended the stairs in slow, weary steps, and knocked on the door with the last ounce of strength in his body. Then the door opened. Colman stood before him.

The lights and the heat hit Coop full in the face. He felt feverish, his chest was heavy, the blood throbbed in his temples. He opened his mouth mechanically, saw the camera spinning around him, and fell flat. Colman caught his head just before it hit the floor.

Colman picked up Coop and carried him to the bed.

"Don't move from there," King shouted to Coop. Then he turned to bark orders to the camera crew to move in for a closeup.

Twenty minutes later the scene was finished.

"OK," King yelled, "you can get up now, Coop, it's all over."

But Gary didn't budge.

"Coop, did you hear me?" King called again.

There was a groundswell of laughter among the grips, electricians, and stagehands.

Coop had fallen asleep.

Sam Goldwyn, who had been watching the scene, ran up to Coop as King shook him awake. "Son," Goldwyn said, "that's the finest bit of acting I have ever seen. You really put yourself into your work."

When the rushes were viewed in the projection room the next day, King knew that Al Goodwin's absence would not be felt. Coop was simply great.

Goldwyn turned to King and asked, "Have we got him under contract?"

"Not yet," King said, "but that won't be for long."

Coop was absolutely flabbergasted. Tired as he was after his exhausting portrayal, he was virtually floating on a cloud when he heard the conversation.

That evening, Gary called his agent to announce that he was going to get a contract.

"That's wonderful," the agent said. "But let's wait them out. Let them get in touch with you. Don't let them think you're hungry."

So Coop waited. But he did not hear from either King or Goldwyn. A week went by. Two weeks. A month. King and Goldwyn, the story goes, had each taken it for granted that the other had signed Coop to a contract. In that month, both were just too busy to bother with contractual matters. They were busy in the cutting room, trimming, editing, and splicing the film they had just finished.

Finally, his agent told Coop:

"Gary, don't let your gratitude to King and Goldwyn keep you from getting the best deal for yourself. If they've forgotten you, then I know somebody who'll give you a contract."

Coop was led straight to Paramount. When they got there, a secretary who had been expecting Gary told him:

"The boss will see you right away — but your agent must wait here for the time being."

Gary went in — right into the office of Paramount's head man, B. P. Schulberg. As he faced this giant of the moving-picture industry and several of his executives who had been summoned to view him, Coop was overwhelmed. He knew that they were all important men; he knew this was his moment of truth — he'd have to make a favorable impression on the brass. It was up to them whether he was signed by Paramount or not.

Coop suddenly felt butterflies twittering in his stomach. His knees became wobbly. He trembled all over. He tried to speak. Nothing. Not a word came out. Struck dumb as he was by the awesome collection of bigwigs, Gary could only gulp and grin embarrassingly.

Schulberg studied the tall, rawboned actor closely, then turned to the others for an opinion. One by one they nodded. One by one they indicated without saying a word that they liked what they saw in the gangling young actor, still too overawed to utter a word.

"How'd you like to work for us?" Schulberg asked finally after the visual poll of his execs. "We're offering you a term contract. The pay is very good — $150 a week."

The shock of Schulberg's words rendered Coop senseless. All he could do was shake his head and manage to utter a half-whispered "y-y-yes."

In the next few minutes, a contract was brought out, pushed under Coop's nose, and he was told to sign. Still tingling with the excitement of becoming a contract player, Coop forgot to call for his agent in the outer office. With a swish of the pen Gary inked his name to the document and it was all over.

When Coop told his agent what he had done, he was fit to be tied.

"Why the hell do you think I came with you?" the agent screamed. "Don't you know those guys have grabbed you for nothing? What happened to all those big ideas you had about getting the big money that Tom Mix is getting? Don't you know that $150 is nothing?"

Coop looked at the agent with downcast eyes. He realized his error. But he was still thrilled to have won a contract berth with Paramount. A deep incredible joy shook him even if the pay was low. Yet he realized he had goofed.

"Maybe they'll give me a raise," Coop said, "if you go in there and tell them their mistake. ..."

CHAPTER EIGHT

An Actor at Last

Most reviews of *The Winning of Barbara Worth* hardly gave Gary Cooper a tumble. With Ronald Colman playing the part of the sophisticated engineer from the East, out West, and the glamorous Vilma Banky filling the screen with her allure, there was scarcely room for much more than a favorable mention of Coop in the columns. Yet his performance was incredibly good.

One of the few who did note Coop's fine contribution, however, was Hollywood columnist Louella Parsons, one of the first to rave about the lanky newcomer to the screen. In her review Miss Parsons wrote:

"In *The Winning of Barbara Worth*, Miss Banky and Mr. Colman share honors with Gary Cooper, whose portrayal of Abe Lee, the other man in love with Barbara, is something one remembers even after the last reel fades from the screen."

Paramount was quick to take advantage of the possibilities in their new property's talent. They saw what Sam

Goldwyn and Henry King had spotted in Coop — and they were shrewd enough to grab him before Goldwyn and King had a chance to realize that they had let him slip from their grasp. At $150 a week, Paramount knew it had a once-in-a-lifetime bargain.

Paramount immediately cast Coop for the lead in a Zane Grey Western called *Arizona Bound.* The director was John Waters, who had been present in B. P. Schulberg's office when Coop was signed.

For his leading lady, Coop would have no less than blonde, fabulously beautiful Thelma Todd, a vivacious and captivating actress whose presence in the film was enough to assure its success, even if Gary failed to render a satisfactory performance.

"Get yourself packed," director Waters ordered Coop, "we're going on location to get some authentic background in this picture."

"Oh," Coop remarked, "we're going to Arizona."

"Don't be silly," Waters shot back. "We're doing the picture in Utah's Bryce Canyon — best Arizona country you ever saw."

Shooting went along on schedule and after two weeks the company was back in Hollywood for interior shots. Waters reported back to Schulberg that Coop handled his assignment like a pro.

"We've got a real man of the West in this Cooper," Waters said. "He handles a horse like he owns it."

"But can he act?" Schulberg wanted to know.

"Gonna find out this afternoon," the director replied. "Got him doing a love scene with Thelma."

It was easier said than done. Coop, in the first love scene of his movie career, reacted in Thelma Todd's presence just the way any matinee gawker might be expected to act

if he were suddenly thrust into the arms of the enchant-
ingly beautiful actress.

He simply couldn't do it. He froze. His senses left him.
At that critical moment, he was a huge, vacant clod. The
camera stopped whirring when Waters shouted "Cut!"

"You're like a high-school kid at the senior prom," Waters admonished Coop. "You're stiff and you act like
you're scared of Thelma. Relax. Take charge of the girl!"

Little did Waters know that Coop actually had been
infatuated with Thelma Todd and that his nervousness was
not due so much to his inability to handle a girl as it was
his inability to handle Miss Todd. She worked a remarkable spell over men, and Coop was no different than other
men who succumbed to her charms.

Coop finally got by the love scenes by taking Waters'
advice to relax.

The picture was released and Thelma Todd got top billing, with Coop's name directly under hers. Coop couldn't
wait to take his mother and father to the premiere, and it
was a thrilling event in their lives to see their son had made
the grade in Hollywood.

"You've shown good stuff," said Coop's father. "I pre-
dict you'll be a big star some day."

Coop smiled, gulped, and sighed.

"Would you like to tell that to Paramount?"

No need to do that. Paramount could see Coop had the
stuff and they exhibited their confidence in Gary's ability
by immediately casting him in another Zane Grey Western, *Nevada.*

"I suppose," Coop told Waters when he learned they
were leaving for location, "I ought to pack my gear for the
trip to Nevada."

"Yes, Gary, get packed," Waters said, "but we're not

going to Nevada — Arizona happens to have the best Nevada background."

Evelyn Brent was Coop's leading lady, and he found her every bit as beautiful, alluring, and attractive as Thelma Todd. He found it much easier going through the love scenes with Miss Brent by following his director's advice to relax.

And he relaxed right into an offscreen romance with Miss Brent, the first of a series of Hollywood leading ladies to be linked with the tall, bashful, silent Man of the West. Newspaper columnists filed stories about Coop's attentions to Miss Brent, thus putting his name in the gossip department for the first time.

The Paramount flacks saw the possibilities for some free space in the nation's newspapers and fan magazines, and they encouraged the romance with every device at their command. They even planted stories that Coop couldn't sleep nights because Miss Brent was on his mind. It made great reading, and movie fans reacted to the romance with keen interest. Mail began to pour in from all over the country, from fans offering Coop advice on how to handle himself with glamorous, sophisticated Miss Brent.

"I guess," Coop said, "they thought I was some kind of hayseed, incapable of coping with a lady of the world like Miss Brent. I began to wonder about myself — did the fans think I was a hick?"

One afternoon during the filming of *Nevada*, when he returned to his portable dressing room after a day out in the 110-degree desert heat, Coop was surprised to find a stranger waiting for him.

"M'sieu' Cooper," greeted the visitor, "I have zee instructions from M'sieu' Le Directeur Waters who say you must be a master swordsman for zee Foreign Legion in two weeks."

"I'm afraid you're in the wrong desert," Cooper quipped, according to a Paramount executive who later learned of the episode. "The camels and the Sahara," Coop continued, "are over yonder. We're doing this picture with shootin' irons and hosses."

"Oh, non, M'sieu," the visitor persisted. "I have zee right place. M'sieu' Waters say to teach you to fight with zee sword — and I am ready. Come, we 'ave not time to lose."

Surprise. The Frenchman had his signals right. It was Coop who was in the dark. Waters had decided, without notifying Gary, to cast him in Paramount's next epic, *Beau Sabreur*, a sequel to the sensational box-office success, *Beau Geste*, which had starred Ronald Colman. Waters had assigned the Frenchman to be Cooper's fencing coach.

Beau Geste had been one of the truly remarkable films of its time. Fans everywhere pleaded for more action-packed adventures like it. Paramount decided to do a sequel, but it wasn't possible with the same cast because everyone had been killed in the grand finale, the storming of the fort. The studio was forced to line up a new cast for the sequel. Coop was one of those picked.

It was now evident that Paramount felt Gary was on the sensational side. So the pressure was on him to fill the studio's demands as they became increasingly greater.

As soon as work on *Nevada* was completed, orders came to shoot *Beau Sabreur*. Meanwhile, Coop had learned a few points about fencing — especially the finer points — and he was ready to play the role of a French Foreign Legionnaire with some authority. William Powell was the star of the picture.

It was while on his *Nevada* location in Arizona that Coop had learned about foils.

"Waters made sure the Frenchman gave Coop his lessons every night after he had worked all day on the picture," a Paramount source recalled. "It was rough on Coop. The searing heat of the desert took plenty out of him. But Coop was game. Night after night he'd work with his French tutor until he had mastered the art of fencing."

"I never became a Douglas Fairbanks with the sword," Cooper mused, "but with my reach I was able to postpone extermination."

Coop's role in *Beau Sabreur* was not big and his name was near the bottom of the cast. Reviewers again gave him only passing mention.

Without much fanfare and without much plot to work with, Paramount hustled Coop into another fast-drawin' Western called *The Last Outlaw*. His career now was moving ahead briskly and yet despite the advances Coop felt a vague dissatisfaction.

"I was sweating bullets and working my ass off," Coop told a friend in Hollywood once, "but all I got out of it was a lousy $150 a week and complete exhaustion. I wanted to do more than just plug spots in pictures — and I was determined to do it or get out of town."

It was in his next picture, *Wings*, that Cooper came to feel that he had a chance to carve a niche for himself in motion pictures.

Wings was to be an epic air spectacle of World War I, an impressive study of aviators and flying, with thrilling aerial combat scenes, bringing to the screen for the first time the brilliant exploits of America's fighter pilots who flew against the Germans over no-man's-land.

For the first time in screen history, air battles were to be filmed in the air, with the countryside instead of the sky as the background — and this necessitated actual battle conditions on the ground. To achieve this realism, a mile-

and-a-half of Texas country in the vicinity of San Antonio was dug up to create a French battlefield. It took 800 workmen two months to wreck trees, plant shell holes, dig trenches, and unreel barbed wire for the desired effect. But once this was done, the ground was as unsuitable for a landing as any battle-scarred acre along the Marne.

The picture was inspired by director William A. Wellman, a veteran fighter pilot who had distinguished himself in the war as a member of the famed Lafayette Escadrille. He had won the Croix de Guerre with four palm leaves and five citations. Wellman wanted to do one great epic air picture as a tribute to the men who flew the planes,

When Wellman got the go-ahead to make *Wings* he plunged into production with a full head of steam. He cast Richard Arlen as Bruce Armstrong and Buddy Rogers as John Powell, the hero. Arlen had flown for the Canadian Royal Flying Corps during the war, but Rogers didn't know anything about planes.

For the picture's only female starring role, Wellman had signed Clara Bow, the beauty from Brooklyn who was soon to become known as the "It" girl, and who would also soon figure prominently in Gary Cooper's private life.

Coop had no idea he would be called on to work in *Wings* until the studio notified him that Wellman had a part for him. Coop was told to report on location in Tucson, Arizona.

Arlen recalled what happened when Coop arrived:

"Old Long Tack had been told to come to our hotel ready to go out on location with us. We were expected on the set about ten.

"Gary didn't show up until 10:30. The driver tried to hurry him into the car. But Cooper couldn't be stampeded and wanted to know, 'Where do we have breakfast?' And then, with everybody hopping around trying to get him started, he had a nice quiet breakfast of pretzels and near beer.

"It was noon when we arrived at the field and Gary was through with the picture by three and on the train for Hollywood at seven. Figuring he was all washed up in pictures, he said, 'This is the shortest movie career a guy ever had for so long a trip.'

"But Gary's career was far from over. His remarkable performance in *Wings* so impressed the front office that when I got back to Hollywood he was playing opposite Clara Bow in *Children of Divorce.*"

Actually Coop's part in *Wings* was shot in less than two minutes. His role was that of a tough flight instructor who called two green air cadets to his tent. The cadets were Arlen and Rogers. Coop dressed them down, told them they'd have to show more guts if they wanted to fly the way he did. That was the only way they'd become pilots.

Rogers offered Coop a candy bar to ingratiate himself with the instructor, but Coop bit a piece off and threw the confection on his bunk in disdain. Then he walked out of the tent to take off on a flight, which ended in a crash and his death.

In this historic film, sound was dubbed in for the dogfights and the aerial flying scenes — but no voices, for this was early 1927. Al Jolson's *The Jazz Singer*, made later in 1927 by Warner Brothers, was the first film to use speaking or singing voices. But sound effects had been in common use in many films before then, although not to the extent that Wellman employed them in *Wings.*

While Gary's role was inordinately brief, it was one of the most talked-about performances in those early days of movies. It was a picture-stealing scene without precedent.

"There I was," Coop recalled years later, "wearing dusty

infantry shoes, leggings, beat-up khakis, and a long leather flying jacket and helmet, leaving Dick and Buddy in the tent. Only a shadow of the plane could be seen on the screen. Then the shadow came together with another shadow, a second plane. There was a splutter of engines and a sound signaling a crash and doom. The camera caught a bit of the smoking wreckage falling out of the sky, then drifted to focus on Dick and Buddy. They stared at each other so effectively that their reaction at my loss made the audience forget their great acting and concentrate on Gary Cooper — a guy that existed on the screen for less than two minutes."

Movie fans by the millions forgot other episodes in the picture but they remembered "that tall flier who died . . . that what's-his-name. . . . "

But the name was one that they would soon know.

Paramount knew what impact Coop's part would have on audiences when his brief scene was developed and rushed through the projector back in the studio. It was decided that Coop could act, that he wasn't cut out to be just a saddle-burner for "they-went-thataway" oaters.

Furthermore, the studio was beginning to notice that Coop was more than just a mild attraction to women. Fan letters for Gary began to cascade into the studio. Most of the mail was from women — unusual in the case of a cowboy actor. B. P. Schulberg and some of the other Paramount brass decided there must be something about their $150-a-week contract player that titillated distaff movie fans. They decided to try Coop in a different kind of vehicle, a spicy thing, *Children of Divorce.*

It wasn't entirely Paramount's idea to put Coop in this picture. Clara Bow, who had met Coop during his brief stint in *Wings,* took more than a casual interest in him.

When she got back to Hollywood, she suggested that

Coop have a part in her next film, *It*, scheduled to be made just before *Children of Divorce*.

The idea was that movie fans would see Gary for the first time in a suit. If he passed the test, then he might be given a bigger and better part in Clara's next picture, *Children of Divorce*.

Paramount sensed Miss Bow had more than just a passing interest in the towering, taciturn Montanan.

So Paramount said okay, because there's nothing better than a made-to-order studio romance to bring eager audiences crowding up to the box office.

CHAPTER NINE

A Fiercely Jealous "It" Boy

When Gary Cooper strode onto the Paramount set on the first day's work on *It*, he had no way of knowing that he was taking part in the birth of a legend.

"It," a catchword of the Roaring Twenties denoting a sexy, charming, pulchritudinous and exciting personality, had been seized as a title for a motion picture, and its selection proved a ten-strike for the picture's star, Clara Bow. As soon as the film opened in theaters around the nation, Clara Bow and "It" became synonymous: overnight, the flaming flapper with the big brown eyes and breeze-blown red hair became the personification of "It."

Hollywood had had its vamps like Theda Bara, and its femmes fatales like Pola Negri, and its many other notable first ladies such as Mary Pickford, Marie Dressler, Mae Murray, Estelle Taylor, and Constance Talmadge — but none of them ever achieved an exclusive "trademark" such as Clara Bow had with "It." A hundred other vamps and femmes fatales would follow the Baras and Negris as the years went by, but there would never again be another "It" girl.

Gary Cooper was one of the cast, but he shared little if any of Clara Bow's glory in her magnificent moment of triumph. His part in the film was brief, if not obscure, and he emerged with no awards or honors. His role was that of a newspaper reporter who wandered into a tenement scene, made a note on a piece of paper, and wandered out. His name barely made the bottom of the cast of characters, so insignificant was his contribution.

But a few days after *It* was completed, Coop was handed the script for *Children of Divorce*. Coop knew then that he was being given a golden opportunity in a sophisticated film of the jazz age in the hell-bent setting of the Roaring Twenties.

With Clara Bow as the star and Esther Ralston and Hedda Hopper (yes, the same Hedda Hopper who later would become a famous Hollywood columnist) in the picture, Coop would be given maximum exposure in the company of feminine pulchritude. It was a big test.

Coop, playing sleek playboy Ted Larrabee, was thrown into a scene that called for him to walk into a gathering of Park Avenue socialites, stop here and there among the small knots of girls, and casually sip champagne from glasses proffered him.

The first take was a debacle. Coop was so nervous in the presence of so many young women that he spilled cocktails all over their dresses and himself. Makeup men spent hectic hours drying off the cast.

Adela Rogers St. Johns, who wrote the screen play for *Children of Divorce*, recalled that Gary's legs "vibrated like a tuning fork" when he strode back and forth in the room.

Coop really fell apart when he had to walk up to Clara Bow and chuck her under the chin.

Hedda Hopper, who was very near when this happened, remarked years later:

"For the first time in his life, Gary was called upon to play a love scene (with a glamorous star like Clara Bow), which was the hardest thing he had ever attempted." [Hedda had overlooked Coop's earlier but similar experience with Thelma Todd in *Arizona Bound*.]

Pete Martin reported that Coop "was the most inept screen lover who ever reached for a pliant waist, and his effort to seem sexy was the most grinding ordeal of his life."

"I couldn't make love to a girl with a camera snooping at me," Gary told Martin. "It just didn't seem decent, especially with a girl I hardly knew."

Frank Lloyd, who was directing *Children of Divorce*, was at his wit's end by the time evening arrived. Every take had to be discarded. The entire day's shooting had been wasted.

The following day, Coop noticed that the scene had attracted some interesting spectators to the stage — B. P. Schulberg, production general manager Walter Wanger, and several other people from the front office. To Coop it looked like an ominous meeting. He saw them in heated conference with director Lloyd.

"I could feel it in my bones that they were talking about me," Cooper said. "They weren't taking the production losses too lightly. I was costing them money and I had a feeling they were rapidly coming to a decision to dump me."

Coop finally managed to get through the scene without spilling any champagne, but it wasn't a performance anyone raved about. He appeared too stiff, too tight, hardly what a sophisticated man-about-town was expected to look like on the screen.

Hedda Hopper, who had sensed Coop's awkwardness before the cameras, edged up to Gary and tried to offer him some encouragement.

"Don't let it get you down," she said. "You're improving with every take."

Indeed, why shouldn't Coop have improved? As Miss Hopper later related, it took twenty or twenty-one retakes to complete that one scene of Coop amidst the sophisticated young ladies.

Coop had a feeling that Lloyd and the big boys had had their fill of him.

He was half right.

Schulberg and the other Paramount brass ordered Coop yanked out of the picture. Lloyd, however, protested so vigorously that Gary was allowed to come back. The change of heart was prompted by this promise by Lloyd: "I'll make an actor out of him or kill him."

But after a week of sweat and grief in trying to convert Coop into a believable Ted Larrabee, Gary was bounced out of the picture once more. Once more Lloyd protested. Again he got his protégé reinstated. Gary was fired and rehired seven times.

By now, Coop realized it was just a matter of time before the bigwigs lowered the boom again — for good. He decided to beat them to the punch. He took it on the lam, convinced he was a flop.

Gary jumped into his car and drove down Highway 101 to San Diego to get away from it all, then went off into the desert to hunt for a couple of days. On the third night he wearily returned to Hollywood and headed out to Malibu. He spent the night on the beach, walking. The next morning he went back to the vicinity of the Paramount lot and drifted into a restaurant where everyone from the studio met for lunch. He had made up his mind by now. It was all a big mistake, this idea of being an actor. What he should have done in the first place was follow his original desire to study art.

As Gary walked in, the crowd hadn't yet arrived. He sat at the counter and ordered the specialty of the house. He was working his way through the second third-acre of medium-rare steak when suddenly he was rudely knifed in the ribs by an elbow belonging to someone who had taken the next stool.

It was Frank Lloyd. Someone had spotted Coop in the eatery and rushed to the studio to summon the director, who had been beside himself waiting for Gary to return from his disappearance act.

"You've let me down," Lloyd told Coop. "I told them I could make an actor even out of you."

Coop was dubious of his chances of success but relented and went back.

After several days of filming, during which Coop seemed to gain new confidence in himself, he was approached by Clara Bow one afternoon close to quitting time.

"Gary," she said, "I have an idea . . . really it isn't mine. It's Hedda's."

Coop listened with interest.

"Hedda and I agree that the thing that would help you most of all in getting confidence before the cameras is publicity."

Gary wasn't getting the message, and justifiably so. Clara didn't explain what kind of publicity. Perhaps wisely she withheld the details. She knew if she revealed what she had in mind right there on the set, Coop might have gotten cold feet and taken another run-out powder.

"Come on," Clara said, "we'll pick up Hedda and talk about it over dinner."

Coop was stunned when he finally learned what Clara and Hedda had cooked up — not for dinner but for the publicity buildup.

"You're awfully shy," Clara told Coop. "You don't have that sophisticated quality about you. You're giving people the impression that you're a country boy."

"But I am a country boy," Coop protested.

"Yes, but if you want to be a good all-around actor, you've got to shake the hayseed out of your hair. Otherwise you'll always be a cowboy."

"What can I do?" Coop asked, wondering whether Clara Bow — one of the top actresses of the time — might offer some sage counsel about how he might improve his acting.

"Publicity," interrupted Hedda, who was sitting on Clara's left. "Publicity," she repeated.

There it was again — the word that he'd heard before from Clara. What was it all about? What did they mean?

"You've got to get around town," Clara said. "Be seen everywhere — in night clubs, at premieres, you know . . . "

"Will that help my acting?" Coop wondered.

"Yes, it'll give you self-assurance," Clara replied. "People will look at you with admiration, and that will build up your ego. Then you'll face the cameras confidently. Your acting will improve a thousandfold."

"But who'll take notice of me at these places?" Gary asked. "I've already been to some of them and nobody even looked at me."

"They will from now on," Hedda offered. "How can people *not* take notice of you when you'll be Clara's escort? . . . "

"Clara's escort?" Coop was amazed.

"That's right," Clara pitched in. "We'll go to places and do things together. We'll become an 'item'."

Coop was overwhelmed. At first he tried to protest. But Clara and Hedda wouldn't hear him out. They insisted the idea was sound, the objective laudatory, and the prospective gains too promising to spurn a try at it.

Of course, what Coop didn't know was that the studio flacks were right in the thick of the plot cooked up by Hedda and Clara, but had kept themselves in the background because they knew Gary would never have gone along with the scheme if he thought for a moment the movie people were generating the momentum for the phony romance.

"Well," Coop finally relented, "I'll go along for a little bit, but if I see myself falling flat on my face, or spilling cocktails over Clara — I won't continue it."

"Agreed!" Clara and Hedda cried in unison. The ladies then leaped on Coop and playfully rumpled his hair, telling him he was "just wonderful."

If Hollywood historians had taken a poll of up-and-coming actors of those days, they probably would not have found another man around town who would have hesitated to go for the idea as long as Coop did. Publicity is what any young actor or actress needs. And who could have brought Coop or any other actor into the limelight more than the effervescent Clara Bow?

But that was Gary Cooper in 1927 — shy, retiring, slow on the draw in the ways of Hollywood.

There was nothing subtle in the way "Operation Buildup" got underway. Hedda Hopper, whose sense of timing with the columnists was uncanny, arranged for little paragraphs and sticks of type about Gary and Clara to find their way into newspapers with almost daily frequency. And to Gary's horror, the stories began referring to him as the "It" boy.

Later on, Gary would wince when thinking back to those days. His friends ribbed him: "Well, well, so the rugged man of the West has become the 'It' boy, eh?" Coop hung his head in shame. But he had sense enough, along with the courage it took, to stand up against the jibes, to know that the campaign was paying off.

Throughout the publicity campaign, work continued on *Children of Divorce.* Lloyd had the most work cut out for him.

Because Coop's long, lean legs continued to tremble like cottonwoods in a high breeze, Lloyd was forced to shoot all Coop's scenes showing only his head and shoulders. He put Coop behind every conceivable prop he could bring in front of the camera — tables, chairs, any piece of furniture that would conceal the bony underpinnings. He even garbed Coop in long bathrobes and polo coats to hide the trembling legs; he had Coop sit through the scenes.

"No actor ever played so many scenes sitting down as Gary did in *Children of Divorce,*" commented the picture's author, Adela Rogers St. Johns.

But Lloyd's troubles with technical matters of filming were not the only ones that plagued him on the set.

The days and weeks rolled by, and still Gary Cooper, the "It" boy, and Clara Bow, the "It" girl, continued their studio-steered romance. Then suddenly, the romance seemed to generate new steam, new force — without any further assistance from Hedda or the studio flacks.

Coop had fallen for Clara.

Now Lloyd was in trouble. Not so much because Gary and Clara were in love but because, like many other young people in love, they began to have spats and fights.

One day, when Coop showed up for a scene, Lloyd flipped.

"How the hell can we shoot you now?" the director shouted.

Coop looked at Lloyd, embarrassed.

"Maybe makeup can fix it up," Gary said, putting his hand up to his eye, all blue and purple.

"Clara's got a hard right," Gary said sadly.

Their reconciliations were not quite as noisy as their battles, but they took place in full view of everyone on the lot — and they held up filming every time.

"That extracelluloid romance," said Miss St. Johns, "must have cost the studio $100,000 in time lost."

Children of Divorce was finally completed and began its bookings around the country. Despite Clara Bow's appearance in it, and Gary Cooper's emboldened performance, despite the buildup, it didn't send the reviewers racing off to compose wild symphonies of praise.

The film reached New York for a first-run showing at the Rialto on Broadway in April, 1927. It got a so-so reaction at best. The New York *Times* review was one of the kinder ones.

"Although there are a number of scenes in *Children of Divorce*, the current film attraction at the Rialto, which are cleverly directed," the reviewer stated, "the narrative as a whole is sluggish and unconvincing at important junctures. But in spite of its tendency to ramble, this film succeeds in holding the attention, thanks to the excellent lighting effects and to the presence of Esther Ralston and Clara Bow . . . ."

"Miss Ralston does very well as the beautiful Jean. Miss Bow is pretty and active as Kitty. . . ."

And down in the very last paragraph of the review came this tidy, capsuled judgment of a couple of other performances:

"Gary Cooper and Einar Hanson, the younger male elements in this feature, give an interesting account of themselves."

Well, at least he got *some* notice.

The romance flourished for months after Gary and Clara finished *Children of Divorce.* Coop was the bashful but always-smiling, always-present escort. The "It" boy and the "It" girl were a constant newspaper item.

But in the course of their romance, Miss Bow was not entirely disposed to give Gary her undivided attention. Other men, Hollywood personalities, were seen in her company in nightclubs and restaurants. But Coop remained stuck on Clara.

Everybody noticed it. One Hollywood lady of prominence, recalling Coop's attachment to Clara, remarked:

"His helplessness as a screen lover had nothing to do with his ability to conquer a woman's heart offscreen. Gary had all the physical attributes of a dashing Romeo, despite his shyness, and I think he knew what magical qualities he had which made women flip over him.

"But I don't think Clara was disposed to lose her head over Coop. She was swamped with offers for dates, and many of the swains were even more attractive in some ways than Coop was. Remember — Clara had the world at her feet. She could snap her finger and any man would run to her, a slave to her whim and fancy for as long as she wanted him.

"What chance did Coop have?"

Since the imaginary romance — drummed up by Clara and Hedda, and abetted by studio publicity agents — turned into a red-hot one-sided love affair, it's understandable that Clara's interest in other men riled Gary.

There were times when Coop sulked and became moody when he tried to date Clara, only to learn she had made other arrangements for the evening that did not include him.

In reporting on the romance, society columnist Igor Cassini said that Clara and Gary had many arguments during the course of their "engagement," and that it was Clara who "did most of the pursuing."

As the symbol of Hollywood in the Jazz Age, a gal who did her best to live up to that position, Clara gave extravagant parties, often with a footman stationed behind each chair at the dining table — with Gary occupying the host's chair, for at least as long as their "engagement" lasted.

The records and Hollywood sources indicate Clara did not exactly toss Coop over like a hot potato. She continued to see him for a good long time and Hollywood gossip columnists persisted in reporting that the Cooper–Bow romance would wind up in a wedding.

It didn't, of course.

It came to a finish one day with Clara's announcement to a film city correspondent:

"Gary and I could never marry. We wouldn't be happy. He's too fiercely jealous!"

And so, as the violins played on, Gary and Clara drifted apart. But to Gary's consternation, his reputation as the "It" boy lingered.

CHAPTER TEN

Lupe Velez—Romance With a Spitfire

The air filled with the angry whine of low-flying dive bombers. They came screaming into the valley, shivering the treetops with the violent wash of their props. Down on the ground, a lean, haggard man placed his arm around the waist of a beautiful forlornly lost young woman and then turned his face upward, silently cursing the peril above, his eyes blazing. Both faces, hers wraithlike in its beauty, his gaunt with weariness, were dirt-smudged and coated with sweat. Above, behind, and all about them, the dive bombers howled in fury; and off in the distance, great scoops of earth flew skyward as the first of the deadly bombs began crashing to the earth. For the moment, all the evil and destructive power of World War I seemed to be contained and concentrated in that one hellish valley. Together, the man and woman turned their eyes toward the horizon and poised there motionless, as though waiting for something . . . waiting . . . and then it came.

"All right, all right, cut! Jesus Christ, Joe, my four-year-old kid can dig better bomb craters with his little goddam pail and shovel."

For a brief time, anyway, Gary Cooper and Fay Wray could leave the scarred and bleeding ground of a war-torn valley and return to their dressing rooms for coffee and sandwiches.

Coop had begun work on *The Legion of the Condemned* and, as he often related years later, he was indeed working his butt off in that hectic era of film making.

Everything combined to make it hectic.

He was still licking the wounds of his broken romance with Clara Bow, but additionally the physical work for an actor at the substar level in that time was grueling and, if not exactly life-endangering, certainly abundant with hazards. Coop was not yet the fabulously salaried star he was to become in a few years, so he still didn't merit the lavish expense of a stunt man. The results were sometimes a bit grotesque.

In *The Legion of the Condemned* and in the film that followed it, *Doomsday,* Coop was sent into action scenes that involved exploding land mines, bursting air bombs, and bone-jarring underwater explosions. But the concussion of studio-created blasts wasn't the only hazard that periled Coop in those still rather primitive, or at least unrefined, moviemaking days.

The amount of work became a grind. It was a welcome grind, perhaps, but the schedule of Gary Cooper films became tighter and tighter and made more and more demands on the fast-rising star.

By this time the pressure on him — which had begun with preparations for *Beau Sabreur* — was heavier than ever. Coop was becoming a somebody in movies.

His own method of taking on a role and playing it the way he imagined he would feel and behave in the circumstances of the part was proving a success. Since he was naturally quiet-spoken, shy, and reserved, his characters came out on the screen underplayed.

Some directors would pull their hair out at the lack of pyrotechnics in Coop's acting, and some predicted he couldn't go on too long before he fell flat on his face — a failure. But they underestimated or completely failed to realize that what the eye saw on the movie sets was not the same as the image captured by the camera's lens. On film, Gary Cooper came out just right.

The public liked Coop's confident, relaxed style of acting, his natural, understanding portrayals. The clamor rose for more Gary Cooper films.

In quick succession after *Condemned* and *Doomsday* he was costarred with Colleen Moore in *Lilac Time*, and with Carole Lombard in *Half a Bride*.

Things were happening quickly at that time, in Cooper's life, in Hollywood, and in the world beyond. America was barreling blithely along, full of blind confidence, heedless of the frantic warnings of a few far-sighted prophets, and then it was too late. The great cataclysmic Depression hit with a shuddering jolt, and suddenly the wild, frenetic Jazz Age was over. The Roaring Twenties died, not with a roar but with a thin, frightened whine. The upheaval that accompanied the stock market crash of 1929 was total and felt even in the hitherto insulated precincts of Hollywood.

With the upheaval came a nibbling of fear that now, for the first time since the motion picture industry began, the fluffy pink existence of Hollywood was threatened. The phantom fear lurking in the darkness was radio — the wooden box with the hissing sound — which gave empty-pocketed American families something to do with their time.

Movie box offices everywhere were hurt. Money was scarce, and food came first, and clothing, and rent. A dime that once bought admission into the gaudy cinema temples of Main Street now went for cereal and soup meat. And radio kept everyone — or at least too many to suit the movie industry — at home. Something new and drastic had to be done to draw the people back to the theaters, and everyone knew it could be one thing and one thing only.

Sound.

The talkies.

Hollywood had to fight sound with sound.

The advent of sound rushed in so swiftly it caught many directors and producers completely unprepared. Feverishly, they tried all kinds of gimmicks to save from the scrap pile the silent pictures they had already started.

Gary Cooper was in such a film when Paramount decided it could never be released as a silent movie; the executives decided to make it a sound film. Neither Cooper nor his costar, Nancy Carroll, had ever spoken into the frightening microphones the studios had developed for their talkies.

Coop, in an autobiographical series of articles in the *Saturday Evening Post* in 1956, had this to say about the episode:

"For all of 59 minutes and 45 seconds of its hour-long run, we acted in silence. Then came the final wedding scene. We stood before a minister. I was ready. I had studied my script containing this new thing called dialogue until I was letter-perfect."

Then, Coop related, the dialogue went like this in the final wedding scene:

Coop: "I do."

Nancy: "I do."

"On those four words," Coop declared, "they released the picture as a talkie."

The late Nancy Carroll — who had become a successful television star and Broadway actress, still a sparkler, vi-

brant from the top of her flame-hued hairdo to her trim
ankles, and a grandmother four times over — readily consented to talk about *Shopworn Angel* at an interview with
the author.

"Coop was my favorite leading man," said Miss Carroll,
"and his recollection was all right as far as he went. Those
four words were in the picture all right, George, but there
was more dialogue than that. In fact, there was a song in
the picture too — the first a girl sang on the screen."

It was Nancy Carroll's song: "Precious Little Thing
Called Love."

However small his own speaking part was, Gary's dialogue did make an impression on at least one reviewer.

"If this picture proves nothing else," said the movie
critic, "it certainly assures his fans that Gary Cooper has
a voice and can speak."

That was an invaluable asset to Hollywood actors and
actresses in that critical era. There were many who
couldn't speak; that is, their voices came over the theater
loudspeaker as shrill, scratchy, undistinguishable noise.
Their future as stars in the cinematic firmament was black.

As Coop's popularity began reaching new heights in this
new world of sound movies, his life increasingly became
public property, and, inevitably, the inherently shy actor,
often to his painful embarrassment, found himself grist for
the nonstop publicity mills grinding out news of the Hollywood colony in columns, news and feature newspaper stories, and fan magazine articles.

The newspaper and magazine space that Gary Cooper
and Clara Bow had achieved as the "It" boy and girl was
a mere speck compared with the guff poured out after his
meeting with his next important costar — Lupe Velez. It
began virtually the moment Gary was signed to play opposite Lupe Velez in a tale of the Spanish Southwest in the
1840s, called *Wolf Song*.

Lupe didn't object to the publicity, coming as it did after her dramatic climb to stardom. The exotic Mexican spitfire had flashed, stormed, and sparkled her way to the top. Her appearance on the set was invariably explosive, and she was apt to hurl things around in anger at the slightest provocation. And yet she objected to being called "wild," the tag reporters tied on her.

"I am not wild," she would protest. "I am just Lupe."

When Lupe was teamed by Paramount to costar with Coop, she had just returned from a triumphant appearance in Douglas Fairbanks's production of *The Gaucho*, in which she achieved considerable distinction with her interpretation of a termagant. Director Victor Fleming brought Lupe into *Wolf Song* to play a more placid but not wiser young woman named Lola Salazar, daughter of a highborn Spanish family. Coop's role was that of Sam Lash, a trapper, who knew no barriers to love.

The plot, quite basic, has Coop finding the window of Lola's bedroom, pleading with her to marry him, running off with her, then deciding their uneventful marriage is tedious. He deserts his bride one morning and returns to a trapper's life and his comrades of the past. He encounters Indians, ducks bullets and arrows, and finally decides to return to Lola. She hates him for having left her, but the pathetic sight of Lash, crawling up to her, causes Lola to throw her arms around the young man's neck.

The review of the film in the New York *Times* on February 25, 1929, found director Fleming "guilty" of the indiscretion of "prolonging a violent kiss until it becomes more absurd than passionate."

Little did the reviewer, or the public for that matter, know then that, to a large extent, the passion and duration of the kisses were very real.

The secret didn't remain a secret long and the publicity hounds soon began to pour out torrents of love notes on

Gary and Lupe, who had started dating.

One episode that received widespread publicity was Gary's gift of a pair of golden eagles to Lupe. The eagles were sent by a fan up in Montana, who read somewhere that Coop was interested in falconry. The sender suggested that Gary try training the birds.

Coop was still living with his folks at home, and there wasn't room in the house for the eagles. But Lupe had a huge backyard in her Laurel Canyon hideaway. Coop decided she wouldn't mind boarding them.

"What you have there, Garee?" asked Lupe in wide-eyed horror when he showed up at the front door with the birds in a steel cage.

"Eagles," Coop said matter of factly, "and they're right friendly ones. Won't give you a bit of trouble."

"Trouble!" the fiery actress screamed. "What you theenk you going to do with those . . . those . . . monsters?"

"Keep 'em in your backyard, of course."

"What? You are . . . you are crazeeee!"

Wild as the idea might have seemed to Lupe, Coop talked her into boarding the eagles. He had a very large cage built in the backyard, and the eagles remained.

Snooping Hollywood reporters found out about the eagles. One headline that topped a detailed story about Gary's gift to Lupe went:

"Coop Gives Lupe the (Love) Bird."

By now Gary and Lupe were more than an "item" — they were virtually inseparable. They were seen together at premieres, restaurants, nightclubs, and other public places. He would go to her house for weekends. Sometimes he would stay there for weeks.

Coop eventually even took Lupe home to meet his folks. Mr. and Mrs. Cooper were both baffled by the fiery Mexican tamale. But it wasn't long before they realized that beneath her sizzling exterior lay a genuine warmth and deep kindness. They also sensed something else — that Lupe not only liked Gary, but loved him.

As for Coop — well, Lupe hit him hard, too, like a tropical hurricane roaring up from the Gulf of Mexico.

Hollywood watched the romance and started to talk. The rumormongers, reporting how much time Coop was spending over at Lupe's place, speculated that they were living there as man and wife, actually married.

Adela Rogers St. Johns described a scene in Gary's and Lupe's life that she had witnessed.

"I came back from swimming one day at Malibu Beach to find Gary sound asleep on the couch and Lupe kneeling beside him. Now I yield to no one in finding Cooper the most attractive man that's ever been in Hollywood, but Cooper asleep and snoring gently with his mouth open is a good deal like any other man asleep and snoring gently with his mouth open. Nevertheless, Lupe looked up at me and said in a voice throbbing with emotion, 'Is he not beautiful? I have never seen anyone so beautiful as my Garee.' "

As Lupe spoke, Gary opened one of his eyes. He had overheard Lupe and was overcome with mirth. Turning swiftly, Lupe caught Coop in the act.

"You laugh at your Lupe's love!" cried the Mexican spitfire.

It turned into a wild, scrambling, knockdown scene in which Coop had to wrestle Lupe down on the couch and hold her there until she cooled off. By then, Coop was worn out.

Coop's and Lupe's peregrinations gave every indication that wedding bells would not be an unlikely outcome of their romance.

But it was a hot-and-cold love affair so far as the outside world was concerned.

"Of course I love him," Lupe would say. "Marry him?

Well, who will know what I do until I do it, eh? Maybe tomorrow, maybe next month, maybe never. But I think maybe."

A few months later, she would say capriciously, "I don't love Gary Cooper. I don't love anybody ... I will never marry. I stay Lupe. I am sick of love."

Lupe seemed to fear marriage. To her it spelled the end of the wild and reckless life she loved to lead.

"I must be free," she would say. "I know men too well, they are all the same, no? If you love them, they want to be boss. I will never have a boss."

There are many who believe Gary felt the same way about marriage in those days.

Although madly in love with Lupe, something inside avoided marriage to the fireball from south of the border. Lupe didn't seem to belong in his portrait of marriage.

But Lupe was more fun than a house full of wildcats.

And while he suffered many lacerations in his encounters with her, Coop continued to keep company with Lupe because, he told himself ruefully, he was still crazy about her.

CHAPTER ELEVEN

"When You Call Me That, Smile!"—A Line to Stardom

After *Wolf Song*, Lupe Velez, a $2,500-a-week star, was plunged at once into another picture, and Gary Cooper, now earning $750 a week, was shoved into another while his publicity was still flaming hot.

The year was 1929 and the picture Paramount chose for its rising young star was *The Virginian*. It was the first major talkie ever filmed outdoors, and the size of the production as plotted by the studio architects was enough to stagger the imagination of moviemakers and fans alike in those early days of sound.

The picture was made in Sonora, in the High Sierras, and it was one of Hollywood's most involved adventures of the day. Not only did Paramount have to transport its stars and cameras to location, but with them rumbled vast truckloads of new paraphernalia — sound equipment.

Cooper's costar was Richard Arlen, who by now had become fast friends with Gary, along with Buddy Rogers. They were known around Hollywood in those days as the "Three Musketeers." **101**

There were many dramatic and interesting scenes in the film, but there were some that never got on film — or at least not the film that movie fans got to see.

There was one scene in which Coop, as the Virginian, had just caught his old buddy, Steve, with a rustled herd of cows. Cooper was to seem heartbroken and express sorrow over discovering his best friend to be a thief. But Coop couldn't remember his lines.

In their tent after a difficult day before the cameras, Arlen approached Coop with an idea.

"Look, Long Tack," he said, "I've got an idea on how you can go through that scene with me without flubbing your lines. I'll jot them down on my chaps. Then all you've got to do is snitch a look at my chaps every now and then and read the lines."

The next day Coop went before the cameras and breezed through the part — perfectly.

In another scene, Coop had a close brush which nearly cost him his nose. It happened when the take boy brought the slate over to indicate the take number as the camera started to whir. But because this was sound, the slate now was equipped with a slapstick — two pieces of wood on a hinge. The take boy's job was to hold up the slate in front of the camera to indicate the number of the take, then slam the slapstick with a loud clack to cue in on the sound track.

Cooper watched calmly as the boy held the slate in front of him. Then, without turning to see what he was doing, the boy let the slate get right on top of Gary and brought the stick down with a violent slap. It was close. Another tenth of an inch and Coop would have had a bleeding, bone-shattered bulb hanging from his face.

He was shaken so badly he blew his lines. And they had to shoot the scene over.

The success of *The Virginian* was instantaneous. Movie

audiences around the country really sat up and took notice of the craggy, noncommittal Cooper, who cast a shadow half again taller than life; all at once they discovered a hero who was slow to anger but quick on the draw. It was a public image that had its roots in Cooper's own nature, and he was quickly hailed as the legitimate successor of William S. Hart and Tom Mix and the other early heroes of Hollywood's alkali flats.

The fans liked the rare realism and authority that he brought to the picture. As few gunslingers before him, Cooper put himself across as the genuine article.

When Owen Wister began writing *The Virginian*, the year was 1901 — the same year Coop was born. It was one of the most satisfying moments in Wister's life when he was able to see his book made into Gary Cooper's first all-talking picture in 1929. Wister's book was really the first "Western," and the novel sold over 1,600,000 copies, creating as it did a whole new concept of the West — and the basic plot for horse operas of the future.

Wister not only brought the West to the people back East in all its color and romance and spirit, but even awakened Westerners themselves to the idea that much of their daily routine was actually romantic. Eating salt pork, herding ornery cattle, and running headlong into desperadoes' bullets suddenly took on new meaning for all America. Wister's hero of the West was a slim, roughhewn, self-effacing Peter Pan, a gunslinger who could ride and shoot and live in the face of danger without batting an eyelash.

"Daring, laughter, endurance — these were what I saw upon the countenances of the cowboys," wrote Wister, who added: "What has become of the horseman, the cowpuncher, the last romantic figure upon our soil? . . . Well, he will be here among us always, invisible, waiting his chance to live and play as he would like. His wild kind has been among us always, since the beginning: a young man with his temptations, a hero without wings. . . ."

Gary Cooper suddenly became that hero, the essence of the cowboy, the spirit of the West, giving real and true meaning to the films he played.

The scene in Chapter Two of *The Virginian* was made to order for Cooper, and he played it so well, so true to the script prepared by the screen writers that his portrayal became the quintessence of cowboyism to all who saw the film. It went almost exactly the way Wister had written it:

"The poker game at the Medicine Bow Saloon; the villain, Trampas, is impatient with the young Virginian, who inevitably takes his time about deciding whether to call, raise, or fold his hand. . . .

Therefore, Trampas spoke: 'Your bet, you son-of-a-b————.' "

"The Virginian's pistol came out, and his hand lay on the table, holding it unaimed. And with a voice as gentle as ever, the voice that sounded almost like a caress, but drawling a very little more than usual, so that there was almost a space between each word, he issues his orders to the man Trampas:

" 'When you call me that, *smile!*' And he looked at Trampas across the table.

"Yes, the voice was gentle. But in my ears it seemed as if somewhere the bell of death was ringing; and silence, like a stroke, fell on the large room. . . ."

Suddenly it was Gary Cooper, the apparition on the screen, becoming the essence of the cowboy as an American hero.

The success of *The Virginian* went a long way toward establishing Coop as a star in his own right.

"The important thing to me at that stage of my career," Coop said, "was that *The Virginian* unshackled me from that tag as the 'It' boy. I was back to being a rugged, wholesome, outdoor man of the West."

If Coop had been a valuable property to his studio before, *The Virginian* made him doubly so. Without rest, he was pushed into starring roles in *Seven Days' Leave, Only the Brave, The Texan, Paramount on Parade,* and *The Spoilers.*

Coop was achieving stature rapidly; the schedule of pictures Paramount was tossing his way proved that, and so did the roster of leading ladies who were being picked to costar with the gangling, good-looking, soft-spoken Gary.

Soft-spoken?

True enough, Gary Cooper was soft-spoken — but in 1930 he wasn't necessarily always the boy with the whispering voice, not by a long shot. This was the new era — the era of sound — and anyone with the wrong decibel rating didn't rate before the hard-of-hearing microphones of the early talkies.

Hundreds of actors from the silent days had suddenly discovered that being able to talk wasn't enough. They had to speak with a booming voice to get recorded on the sound track. Hollywood was firing carloads of silent screen stars, including many of the featured and supporting players who had appeared in films with Cooper. But despite the fact that he was naturally soft-spoken, Cooper came through unscathed, because when he had to, he could yell as loud as the loudest of them.

His days on the Montana ranch stood him in good stead. Up there one of his duties was to holler at the hogs and cattle — good training for him when the chips were down, and the mikes up, on a Hollywood sound stage.

Paramount decided that Coop's performance in *The Virginian* and subsequent films rated his elevation to more noteworthy roles, so he was cast in an adventure film about the French Foreign Legion called *Morocco*. The picture was noteworthy for two important reasons: it involved the importation for the first time in Hollywood history of both a foreign director and a foreign actress. The director was Josef von Sternberg and the actress was Marlene Dietrich.

Marlene and Gary hit it off very nicely but his relationship with von Sternberg soon collapsed into shambles. Gary resented a habit von Sternberg brought with him across the Atlantic and didn't seem desirous of shaking. He tried to direct Marlene through the entire production in German. Marlene, of course, didn't mind at all, but Coop — well, he'd had enough trouble with French and Latin in that English school in Dunstable.

One day Coop decided to shake von Sternberg of the habit. It happened while the director was giving Marlene instructions in their native tongue.

Coop simply yawned — but loudly.

Von Sternberg looked at Gary with fire in his eye.

"Iv you are schleepy you can go to ze home," he said sarcastically.

"Oh, no," Coop replied just as caustically, "it's just that this is America and we don't understand this kraut talk."

According to a Paramount historian who recalled the incident, von Sternberg was fit to be tied.

"Every von go home," he shouted, his face burning with anger. "Ve vill not vork anymore today. I haf been inzulted and I vant to dink dis ovah."

After that, von Sternberg stuck to English.

Paramount was delighted with Coop's efforts in *Morocco*. They gave him top billing with Miss Dietrich, despite von Sternberg's plea to dump Coop's name to the bottom of the cast list.

Coop's promise as a screen star excited the studio, so they halfheartedly tried to do something about his complaint about working too hard. They threw more pictures at him to capitalize on his growing popularity, while offering at the same time to ease up somewhat on the pressure. That was when they told him they had "split up your schedule." They would film one picture in the daytime and another at night. This way Coop could make two pictures at the same time.

The year was 1931. The schedule was racing wildly onward.

More and more pictures, two at a time. Less and less time for himself. Overwork. Fatigue. But Coop continued the backbreaking routine.

While working on *City Streets*, Coop suddenly had to pay the price of overwork. All day he had been up on location in the Hollywood hills playing an Indian fighter in *Fighting Caravans*. A broiling hot sun had sapped him of his strength and energy; that night he rushed into Hollywood to work with Sylvia Sidney in *City Streets*.

Suddenly, while playing a scene with Sylvia, Coop felt faint. The stage began to whirl around. Sylvia noticed Coop turning white. She called the director.

"What's wrong, Gary?" he was asked.

"I guess I'm s-s-sick. . . ."

Coop was sick. He ended up in the hospital.

"This is a clear case of exhaustion, complicated by jaundice," Coop remembered the doctor telling him. "I recommend you stop shooting pictures in pairs — and I also recommend you get as far away from Hollywood as you can for a long, quiet rest."

Coop had just enough punch left to finish the pictures he had been working on, and then he went home to ponder the doctor's advice.

He was lying in bed, and it was past midnight when suddenly there was an eerie, terrifying scratching at the window. The noise not only startled Coop but also awakened his mother and father. They rushed to the window to investigate.

A small crowd was gathered outside, tossing gravel at the window. They were youthful fans who had come to plead with Gary for a personal appearance at the door.

It was too much for Gary. He made two quick decisions. One was that his folks needed their sleep, even if he had to do without his. He decided to move into bachelor quarters. He also thought about the doctor's advice to go as far away from Hollywood as he could. He held off for a while on that decision. First he rented his own place, Greta Garbo's old house. Then he got around to what the doctor had suggested.

He booked passage to Europe.

"I have only one thought," Coop told reporters in New York as he sailed for the Continent. "I want to get as far away from Hollywood as possible. I need rest. I'd like to saddle a gondola and ride off somewhere — anywhere that will provide me with peace and quiet. I crave to be left alone."

It wasn't living in Garbo's house that made Gary Cooper feel the Garbo way. He really was all tuckered out.

CHAPTER TWELVE

The Cowboy Meets the Countess

Venice, the "Queen of the Adriatic," a city whose buildings and statuary express supreme artistic achievement, from Byzantine to Italian Gothic to Renaissance styles, a city rich in the works of Bellini, Giorgione, Titian, Tintoretto, and Veronese. A city of great beauty and tranquility where Gary Cooper got his wish — to be left alone, to be ignored.

"When I went to Hollywood, I had no talent for acting," Coop once told an interviewer about this stage of his career when rest was the only thing he needed and wanted. "I had come to Hollywood full of zip and energy. I was ready to take on any assignment, no matter how rugged. Now I was approaching thirty, not really old — but what energy I had was gone. I felt like an old man. I needed rest and relaxation. Hollywood had burned me out, and I hadn't even begun to act. I felt like tossing in the towel. I was very depressed."

Two weeks of being a happy nobody in Venice. He had

wandered around, relaxed on the white sands of the Adriatic, swum in its glistening blue waters, and ogled the Venetian women. And then, when the two weeks had passed, he was recovered enough to feel lonesome, and to wonder about himself and his future.

On his trip to Europe Coop had been reassured, to a degree, that he was already a somebody. When his boat docked in Algiers, enroute to Italy, Coop came down the gangplank plagued with doubts about himself. By this time he had convinced himself he had no talent as an actor, and that the only thing he had brought to his career in Hollywood was his energy. And now he was certain he had even exhausted that. He felt at the end of his rope.

As he waited around the dock meditating in gloom, a group of little Arab children suddenly gathered around the towering actor, chattering in French. He caught the word "*cinema.*" Then they went charging off. In a few minutes they were back — with fifty more kids. They grinned at Coop, and some of them, contorting their fingers into pistols, pointed them at Gary and yelled, "Boom!" Boom!"

"That made me feel better," Coop said in a ghosted autobiographical sketch in *McCall's* magazine many years later. "At least, I had impressed somebody in this world. My exhilaration carried me to Venice, but when I settled there and nobody recognized me, I began getting depressed again. I wasn't an artist. I wasn't an actor, either. I was nothing more than a hunk of celluloid pieced together in cutting rooms by directors."

Gary Cooper found he really didn't want to be ignored.

While he was lolling about the hotel lobby one afternoon, moping about himself and his career, and cringing at his uncomfortable solitude, he received a letter from Walter Wanger.

"Gary," the letter read, "I think you'll find yourself

getting lonesome by yourself in Venice. . . . I suggest that you take a run down to Rome and visit a friend of mine, the Countess Dorothy di Frasso, who has a place called Villa Madama. . . . I'm sure you'll have an enjoyable time."

Wanger's letter was perfectly timed. Gary, morose with self-doubts and weary of idleness, was anxious for some new and different kind of diversion.

Coop knew nothing about the countess, but he got an idea from Wanger's letter that she was quite a gal. "She runs a sort of open house for celebrities, dignitaries, royalty on the go, and other congenial characters," Wanger wrote. "She'll welcome you with open arms."

Coop decided to visit the countess.

The Countess di Frasso was born Dorothy Taylor, daughter of a wealthy Watertown, N. Y., family. Dorothy managed to keep the golden bit in her teeth at all times, especially after inheriting $12,000,000 from her father, Bertrand Taylor. When she was very young she married Claude Graham White, the famed English aviator, but the marriage was brief, ending in divorce in 1916. In 1923 she married Count Carlo di Frasso, and with her fortune they bought the Villa Madama, a huge estate that had deteriorated through a century or more of neglect and misuse. The ancient villa was really a good-sized palace, but parts of it, containing priceless murals on marbled walls, had been carelessly used as cow barns. The countess had the floors, walls, and murals restored to their former splendor; had installed electric elevators in the sprawling house to save guests from climbing the huge marble staircases; and had hung silk curtains and expensive paintings on the walls.

The countess's friends ranged from Italian nobility to Hollywood greats, and never a day went by that some sizable representative body from these two venerable factions of society wasn't taking advantage of Dorothy's hospitality.

And never let it be said that Elsa Maxwell missed out on the open-door policy. In fact, Elsa was right there when word came that Coop was going to visit the Villa Madama.

"He has a letter from Walter Wanger," the countess told Elsa. "He read in the papers that we were in Naples and said he had an urge to join our party there, but then decided he might be 'butting in.' So now he's coming here. It's his first trip to Europe, apparently, and he's leaving for the villa this afternoon."

"How do you know all this?" Miss Maxwell asked.

"He telephoned," the countess replied. "He has a drawl. Sounds as if he might be a country boy."

"He was born on a range, I believe," Elsa volunteered. "I have read his father was a judge in Montana."

The hostess and her guests were scheduled to leave the villa before Gary's arrival, for they had a horse show to attend in Naples. Word was passed to the servants to expect the visitor.

Cooper arrived at the villa in late afternoon and was welcomed by the butler. In early evening, the countess phoned to see if Gary had been made to feel at home. Coop came on the line.

"Gee," he said, "I didn't know there was a house like this. . . . I'm afraid to walk on the floor. It's made of jewelry. And the frescoes on the walls by that Raphael — who died hundreds of years ago — why, they're so fresh-looking you'd think they were painted only yesterday."

"Tell me," the countess asked Elsa Maxwell after talking with Gary, "what does this Cooper look like?"

Elsa had not met Gary Cooper personally at that time, but she had seen him in *The Virginian.* She had also been told that he was extremely charming. As a joke, she told

Boyhood days on the Seven-Bar-Nine. Young Frank (Gary) Cooper, sitting on the extreme left, entertains his aunts and cousin on a visit

Gary Cooper at the age of sixteen (1917)

Gary's father, Charles H. Cooper, Associate Justice, Montana Supreme Court   *Courtesy Montana Historical Society, Helena*

Getting Even With Their Former Masters

Doc: That's what they are going to get for kicking us off the pay roll.
Joe: But it will not put us back again very soon!

Cartoon drawn by Gary Cooper for the Helena *Independent*, November 2, 1924. It dealt with Doctor Lanstrum and Governor Joseph Dixon, who were involved in a controversial metal mines tax measure   *Courtesy Montana Historical Society, Helena*

Gary and his mother, Mrs. Charles H. Cooper, in Hollywood (1927)

Gary Cooper and Fay Wray in *The First Kiss* (1928)
Courtesy S. Robert Riskin

With Fay Wray (1929)

GARY COOPER AND FAY WRAY WERE BILLED /

Gary Cooper and Fay Wray, in a photograph "autographed" by the
stars and mailed by the Paramount studio to fans *Courtesy J. Hussey*

"ARAMOUNT'S GLORIOUS YOUNG LOVERS"

Richard Arlen   *Courtesy J. Hussey*

Clara Bow   *Courtesy J. Hussey*

Mary Brian

Courtesy J. Hussey

Nancy Carroll

Courtesy J. Hussey

Marlene Dietrich

Courtesy J. Hussey

As The Llano Kid in *The Texan* (1930)

Gary and his father, Judge Cooper

Gary Cooper, at extreme right, shows off a greater bustard, the largest land bird of Africa, which he bagged on safari in 1931

Coop appeared as The White Knight in *Alice in Wonderland* (1933)
Courtesy S. Robert Riskin

With (left to right) Johnny Weismuller; Mrs. Bruce Cabot (Adrienne Ames); Mrs. Johnny Weismuller (Lupe Velez); his wife, Rocky; and Bruce Cabot (1934)

With his older brother, Arthur

Sam Goldwyn and Gary Cooper (1938)

In *The Westerner* (1940)

With the famous war hero, Sergeant Alvin C. York

As Sergeant York (1941)

Edward Arnold and Coop in *Meet John Doe* (1941)

In *Ball of Fire* (1941)

Coop's home was jammed with hunting trophies and rifles

Coop and Rocky (1940)

Coop and Rocky at the premiere of *Meet John Doe;*
seated in back of them: Barbara Stanwyck and Robert Taylor

Gary Cooper and his mother

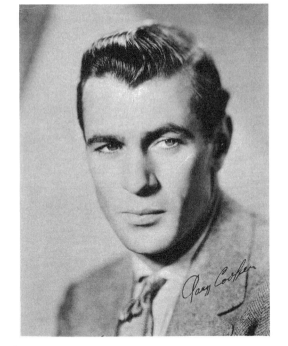

Gary Cooper, 1930   *Courtesy J. Hussey*

In *Pride of the Yankees*, 1942

Gary Cooper, 1940

In *The Naked Edge*, 1961

Seen at a party in the early 40s: Mrs. Gary Cooper, Jack Benny, Gary, Joan Crawford, and Phil Terry, then Miss Crawford's husband

As Lou Gehrig, in *The Pride of the Yankees* (1942)

In *Cloak and Dagger* (1946)

Gary and Rocky at a barn dance

Gary Cooper and Bob Hope are introduced by Danny Thomas, master of ceremonies for a celebrity baseball benefit

Keenan Wynn, Maria Cooper (Gary's daughter), and Gary

Dennis Morgan and director David Butler look on while Cooper studies his one line of dialogue for *It's a Great Feeling* (1949)

In *Task Force* (1949)

In *The Fountainhead* (1949)

In *Bright Leaf* (1950)

In *Dallas* (1950)

In 1957, Coop was photographed at the opening of the Sadler's Wells Ballet in Hollywood

In *The Garden of Evil* (1952)

Gary Cooper and Walter Brennan met when they were both extras in *Watch Your Wife* (Universal, 1925) and remained friends for 36 years

Gary Cooper and Deborah Kerr in *The Naked Edge*, his last film

At the testimonial dinner thrown by the Friars Club on January 8, 1961, when he said, "The only achievement I am really proud of is the friends I have made in this community."

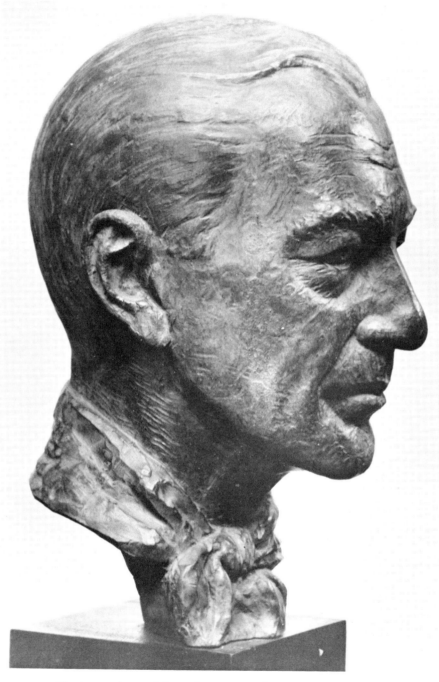

The bronze bust of Gary Cooper commissioned by the Friars Club,
Beverly Hills, Calif.

Courtesy Montana Historical Society, Helena

the countess, "He's a most unprepossessing fellow. Very short. Very plain."

Later that week, the countess and her entourage returned to the villa. As they entered the beautiful reception hall, there stood Coop in all his manly splendor, tall, handsome, and smiling the shy smile that was winning the hearts of women at every matinee performance from Bangor to Beverly Hills.

The countess took one look at Coop, then whirled around to glare at Elsa.

"Elsa Maxwell, you rat," cried the countess, "I might have known you would have your joke!"

The weekend saw the villa fill up with dignitaries just as Wanger had mentioned in his letter. There were Prince Umberto, Woolworth heiress Barbara Hutton, and the Duke of York (later to become King George VI of England), each with his own little clique of friends along to "keep the joint jumping," as Coop later related.

"I was like a little lost sheep in the middle of all that royalty and society."

Countess di Frasso instantly realized that Gary Cooper might not feel too comfortable with the sophisticated crowd she had invited.

"I imagine he might enjoy a session with the Italian cavalry," the countess suggested to Miss Maxwell. "Shall we give it a try?"

Elsa thought it was a peachy idea.

The Italian cavalry she invited consisted of a colonel and nine of his finest horsemen.

The colonel was a man who held the capabilities of his riders in high esteem, and when he learned Gary Cooper was a horseman from the American "Wild West" he took particular delight in putting the visitor to a test against his own riders.

"Eetsa tough course," the colonel told Coop in describing a steeplechase circuit that he wanted the actor to try out. "But I no think you gonna have too much trouble. You cowboys all time ride over da rough ground, no?"

Coop didn't like the tone of voice. There was something in the way the Italian cavalry officer was offering the invitation that made Gary infinitely suspicious. However, he had no alternative but to accept.

"It was more like a challenge," Gary remembered. "He was saying, 'All right, pantywaist, now let's see what you Hollywood cowboys can do against us rugged Romans.' I had to accept."

Coop's suspicions were justified. The course turned out to be the famed Tor di Quinto — one of Europe's toughest. Instead of wooden bars on the hurdles, the Italians had solid stone walls.

"When we started to go," Gary said, "I knew right off that I had no choice but to clear those barriers. If my horse had kicked one of those fences, I'd have been dead."

Coop's days on horseback at the Seven-Bar-Nine, and his experience riding as an extra in those early two-reelers, enabled him to uphold the reputation of Hollywood cowboys in magnificent style. Only the colonel and two of his cavalrymen finished the course — and Gary Cooper.

"Heez very good on da horse, Contessa," reported the colonel when they returned to the villa. The Countess di Frasso was thrilled. She was so proud of Coop's achievement that she quickly spread the word to all her friends — including Walter Wanger in Hollywood. When Paramount got drift of Coop's antics, it decided his health had returned to him. And that called for a back-to-work movement.

RETURN TO NEW YORK AT ONCE TO BEGIN WORK ON NEW PICTURE HIS WOMAN, read the cablegram to Coop.

His costar was to be Claudette Colbert.

In August, 1931, Coop bade the Countess di Frasso a fond farewell, invited her to visit him in Hollywood, if she ever got around that way, and sailed for New York.

When he arrived, Coop found New York bogged down in the grip of a heat wave. At that time, Paramount had a studio in Astoria, across the East River from Manhattan. A carry-over from the pre-Hollywood days of the silent film when movie production was centered in New York, its stages were huge, echoing caverns, totally unsuited for sound productions. But the studio technicians solved the acoustics problem by insulating the sets with padding to drown out echoes. This padding consisted of hundreds of woolen and cotton blankets, bedspreads, ragged quilts, even old rugs. Anything that would cushion noise and improve acoustics was used. Below the hanging padding were dozens of huge spotlights, pouring out a hellish heat.

Under these conditions — lights, suffocating padding, and unbearable heat — Coop soon began to feel his jaundice returning. What strength he had regained in Europe was quickly sapped away, and even his habit of snatching shuteye between scenes on the set helped very little.

Richard Arlen once talked about Gary's sleeping proficiency on the set; he happened to discuss it with a columnist who twisted Dick's words around and made it sound as if a producer had tried to get Coop thrown off his picture for sleeping on the set all the time. Of course, there had never been any such incident. What Arlen did say was:

"Coop had a marvelous knack of being able to sleep when he had to stay on the set while they were shooting something that had nothing to do with his part. . . ."

Dozens of actors and actresses who have costarred with Coop have told similar stories and all have been amazed at the way Coop could stretch out on the set and doze off.

Working on *His Woman*, Coop found that by curling up on a pile of blankets that hadn't been strung up as sound-proofing, he could endure the strenuous conditions under which he had to work. Even so, he was barely able to last it out.

During the filming, as Coop continued to wilt and droop, Claudette Colbert couldn't help noticing how ill Gary looked. She asked what was wrong, and Gary proceeded to explain about his health.

"Have you seen a doctor?" Claudette asked.

"Every day," Coop replied. "If I hadn't, I'd have collapsed long ago."

The doctor's diagnosis of Coop's condition was jaundice complicated by anemia. Gary was in extremely bad shape — his weight dropped from 180 to 150. He needed rest desperately.

Coop relayed the doctor's prognosis to the Paramount high brass. One of the executives, whom Gary would not name, told him:

"My dear Gary. If you were strong enough to ride with the Italian cavalry and to play around with the Countess di Frasso and her fast crowd, there's nothing you or your doctor can say to convince us that you're not ready to do another picture for us. We want you back in Hollywood, pronto."

Coop balked, but the studio threatened to bring action for breach of contract. Coop wasn't frightened in the least. He had made up his mind to take another rest.

Claudette Colbert also needed a rest. There's a story that made its rounds after shooting on *His Woman* was completed.

Ordinarily, Coop was a mass of pointed elbows and pointed knees, but now, in New York during this strenuous time of his life when his weight was way down, Coop's joints were especially sharp.

One of the scenes in the picture required Claudette to sit in Coop's lap; it took most of the day to shoot the scene. When it was over, Claudette got up, rubbed her aching derrière, and remarked, "Mother should have told me there'd be days like this."

Coop's wish to take a rest came sooner than he expected. Returning from his doctor's office one day shortly after he had seen the last of the Astoria studio sweatbox, he was pondering his troubles with Paramount when he ran into Jimmy and Willie Donahue, a couple of Barbara Hutton's relatives, whom Coop had met while at the Countess di Frasso's Villa Madama.

The Donahue boys were cooking up an African safari and invited Coop to join them. Coop regretfully declined. A few days later, Gary bumped into Jerome Preston and his wife, friends of the Donahues. The Prestons invited Coop to dinner, and there he began to recount his troubles with the studio.

The Prestons listened sympathetically. They talked about their ranch in Tanganyika where they bred horses, and finally Jerry Preston said:

"Look, Coop, we're going on the safari that Jimmy and Willie mentioned to you. We'll be leaving in a few days. Why not come with us? It'll be a fine place for you to recuperate."

The combination of Africa, ranching, and horses was too much to resist. Coop grabbed the earliest boat and sailed for the Dark Continent.

Coop's abdication of his Hollywood responsibilities created an immediate vacuum that the moguls at Paramount, Coop learned in short order, were quick to fill. At the moment, soothed by the prospects of sun, of life in the vast wild stretches of a land still largely untouched by civilization, Coop couldn't have cared less.

And, aside from whatever pleasures awaited him in

Africa, he was entirely too ill to worry about his Hollywood career.

Gary Cooper left for Africa in the early fall. Within a week he lost the dull listlessness in which his illness had shrouded him. Within a month he was definitely on the mend, and by December the jaundice had practically disappeared. If he wasn't yet ready to wrestle a lion, at least he was feeling well enough to cut loose in the saddle to hunt wild animals.

Coop's aimless wandering amid the lush and beautiful plains and forests of Central Africa and the exhilarating adventures of the hunt, however, came to a sudden halt.

The Countess di Frasso, having blasted off from her Villa Madama launching pad, soared into full orbit and landed in Africa, right smack on the Preston ranch.

"Dahling, how delightful to see you again," she said as she greeted Coop on the Preston's veranda. "There," she gushed, planting a kiss on Gary's cheek. "Now tell me, dear boy, you're glad to see me too."

Gary grinned shyly. "Yup," he said. "I sure am."

Along with the countess came her entourage. A safari was quickly organized and the party was off into the wilds. Word of Coop's adventures quickly reached the States. Paramount was fit to be tied. It decided to get even with Coop.

Meanwhile, back at the ranch, the friendship between Gary Cooper and the Countess di Frasso flourished in the wild luxuriant jungles by day and the cozy tent camps by night. Rumors of a romance between them were inevitable.

Back home, newspaper editors, intrigued by the volatile mixture of the Montana-born Hollywood actor camping in the jungle wilds of Africa with the New York-born Italian countess, rushed into print an endless string of stories depicting the torrid love affair. Just how many of the stories were true, and to what degree, is something for the idle thinkers of the world to ponder. Neither Coop nor the countess, hounded by the ubiquitous newsmen, discussed their relationship with anyone. Nevertheless, through what in a later day would be called security leaks, some allegedly valid information reached the reporters indicating that Coop and the countess occasionally found diversions other than swatting tsetse flies. And these stories maintained Coop's public image while away from Hollywood.

Coop loved the openness of the wide, wild country and the smell and taste of freedom — freedom from the fixed, rigid schedules of movie production, from the silly, often outlandish duties required of him by the publicitymongers, from the penned-in feeling that Hollywood seems to impose on its inhabitants.

The long rest had a distinctly salubrious effect on Gary Cooper. Not since his days on the Montana ranch had he felt so completely healthy. And now it was time to head for home.

In Rome, Coop promptly encountered several acquaintances from Hollywood, and despite the disdain he had shown for the film capital the previous autumn, he was now genuinely curious about the effects of his absence. Had the studio bosses wrung their hands in despair? Had they been waiting with petulant impatience for his return? Would they — as he fancied they might — offer him some fantastic new contract with unbelievable concessions? In a word, had he really been found to be indispensable?

The answer was a thundering no. He had created a vacuum, all right, but Hollywood, like nature, abhors all vacuums and Paramount immediately cast about for someone to replace Gary Cooper.

And Paramount had its surprise all ready to spring on Coop — his replacement.

Gary learned that the actor's name was Archibald

Leach, that he was discovered in London, brought to Hollywood, and renamed.

"So what's his new monicker?" inquired Gary of the acquaintances he met in Rome.

"Cary Grant," was the reply.

"Cary Grant!" exclaimed Gary. "Why, that's forgery! They've taken my initials and given them to a guy who's gonna take the bread and butter away from me. How do you like that?"

Then Gary was told that Cary also could act.

"Ouch!" cried Coop. "That finishes me."

But Coop soon learned the picture wasn't as black as he thought. His long safari in Africa and the constant reportage on his romance with the Countess di Frasso had brought him a wealth of publicity — some as wild as the jungles he had just left. And Coop knew enough to make the most of it.

When the newspapers shot reporters down to the Villa Madama to interview Coop, he poured it on about his African adventure.

"Well, now, did I tell you about that wild hippo who came chargin' at me? . . ."

That was the typical beginning of an interview with one reporter. In another, Coop would lay it on thick in describing the way he tussled with an elephant, or a lion. It made good reading back home. It also made Coop an even bigger hero than he had been when he left the states. Picture fans began to wonder when Gary would return. Mail poured into Paramount from the faithful moviegoers, curious to know what Gary Cooper's next picture would be. Paramount sensed its obligation to the public. It also sensed that it could not fulfill this obligation without Gary Cooper. Frantic messages were beamed to their wandering star.

But Gary wasn't receiving them. He was on the go again.

The Countess di Frasso had decided that spring on the Riviera was a time to celebrate. She organized another safari and, with Coop tagging along as a charter member, they embarked on what historians of the time have labeled "a wild reckless safari to the Mediterranean's lushest watering spas."

In the process, Coop became the epitome of the Continental gentleman, thanks to the countess. The rumor was that Dorothy was teaching Coop how to dress and even buying his wardrobe.

Elsa Maxwell confirmed the story that the countess bought Coop's clothes. Said Miss Maxwell:

"Dorothy told me she took his clothes in hand at the very beginning. There was a very good men's tailor in Rome. She took Gary there, ordered him dozens of suits. Apparently, at that time, sartorially speaking, Mr. Cooper was not what you would call smart.

"I remember one item she spoke of particularly. He wore an old-fashioned dangling watch chain extending from his waistcoat button with a locket. She removed that immediately."

In desperation, Paramount finally cabled one message that Coop could ill afford to ignore.

OFFERING YOU NEW CONTRACT TWENTY-FIVE HUNDRED DOLLARS A WEEK ALL CONTINGENT ON YOUR RETURN AT ONCE.

The dispatch hit Coop right in the spot where he had been hurting the most — his pocketbook. Unknown to everyone else, Coop had unloaded thousands of dollars on the long African safari and on the endless parties up and down the Mediterranean coast, and at no time in that freewheeling period had he earned a cent.

His moment of truth came on a return swing through Monte Carlo in the spring of 1932.

"Yup, I was dead broke," Coop said, "flat as a pancake.

I had just enough to pay my fare home. I announced my departure in a way that would permit me to leave without anyone knowing that I was down on my you-know-what."

The countess, of course, tut-tutted the idea and wouldn't hear of it. But Cooper, pleading urgency, pecked her on the cheek and promised an early return. He was given a smashing farewell party one night and was aboard a transatlantic liner the next day, bound for New York.

"I smiled for all the world to see that I didn't have a care in the world," Coop said. "But in truth, inside me, I was scared — real scared. I had no notion of how Paramount would deal with me for my prolonged absence — despite the cable they sent me.

"Being broke left me weak and at the mercy of the studio. I was worried as hell that they'd find me out. . . ."

Broke he may have been, but friends he was not without, because, despite the farewell party for Coop, despite the tearful goodbyes, despite the many parting kisses, the Countess di Frasso was right there on the boat, going back to America with him!

Gary Meets His Wife

Enroute to New York, Gary Cooper had plenty of time to think about his future. Although he was broke, the morrow looked promising. Paramount was eager to have him back — despite all its efforts to supplant him with Cary Grant.

"Must be," he told himself, "I'm really in demand. Perhaps now I can work out a contract with the studio that will be more to my liking — with lots of rest between pictures." Those were Coop's thoughts as the ship brought him to America's shores.

If Coop had hoped to slip quietly and unobtrusively into New York, he didn't know the tenacious quality of the New York press.

Every paper in town had its legmen and photographers at dockside waiting for his liner to berth. With the next editions, millions of readers knew that Big Coop had hit town — and that the countess was at his side.

Within hours, Coop's Hollywood colleagues heard he had returned, and the invitations to dinners, to parties, to weekends at Southampton and Newport began finding their way to him at his midtown hotel.

But the first invitation that Gary — and the countess — accepted was to dine with Elsa Maxwell in the Sert Room of the Waldorf-Astoria, where Miss Maxwell was living. The guests included David O. Selznick, director George Cukor, and Constance Bennett.

"Gary was a darling to accept," said Miss Maxwell. "I know they were in a hurry to get out to Hollywood."

Miss Maxwell, who had never been to Hollywood at that time, was suddenly taken aback during a conversation at the table when the countess said to her, "Elsa, why don't you come out to Hollywood?"

Coop reacted enthusiastically.

"Yes, Elsa, why don't you?" he said.

"Oh, come on, Elsa," said the countess, "and you can stay at Gary's place."

Gulp!

That was Coop, swallowing.

"Yes, Elsa, you can stay at my place," Coop echoed rather weakly.

"I'd love to come," Miss Maxwell put in, "but I have to work for a living."

"Well, get a job out there — you know a lot of people in Hollywood," Dorothy persisted.

Connie Bennett, who was to star in Selznick's film of Somerset Maugham's *Our Betters*, instantly turned to Selznick and said:

"David, why don't you engage Elsa in some advisory capacity on the picture?"

"A wonderful idea," Selznick replied. "Would you do it for $500 a week?"

Elsa nearly choked on the olive in her martini. Of course

she accepted, and agreed to leave in two weeks.

Coop and the countess headed for Hollywood almost immediately — but not before Coop accepted an invitation to a party given by one of Hollywood's most celebrated art directors, Cedric Gibbons.

It was the most important party he ever attended in his whole life.

As he moved through the elegant Park Avenue apartment, drink in hand, stopping first at one clutch of people then another, Coop noticed a tall, beautiful young woman. And she was watching him.

"Who's the brunette?" he finally asked a friend.

"Which one?"

"That one?"

"That's Sandra Shaw . . . wants to be an actress . . . hasn't done anything yet but has hopes . . . you know how these society babes are."

"Society . . . mmmmm."

"Want an introduction?"

"Don't make it too obvious — remember the countess is around."

The introduction was casual. In the ensuing conversation, Coop told of his recent exploits in Europe. Miss Shaw told him her real name was Veronica Balfe, that her stepfather was Paul Shields, a Wall Street stockbroker, and that her uncle was Cedric Gibbons, their host for the evening.

As they stood there, Coop began feeling vaguely uncomfortable. The veneer of poise he had acquired during his flight as an international playboy seemed to vanish and, surprisingly, he found he had nothing to say.

And, certainly, there was the Countess di Frasso to consider.

Well, after all. . . .

The meeting ended on an awkward note, but not before they had spoken briefly and vaguely of seeing each other — perhaps — in Hollywood. Coop would be leaving in a day or two. She'd be heading for the Coast at some hazy date in the future.

Gary Cooper's immediate problem centered on negotiations for his new contract with Paramount. Gary knew precisely what he wanted. What's more, he knew exactly how he'd present his demands. He knew he was broke and therefore at the mercy of the studio. On the other hand, the important thing was that the studio didn't know it. Paramount had cabled him a plea to come back and offered him $2,500 per week. He decided to throw caution to the winds and present his demands, bold as brass.

When he arrived in Hollywood, he found Paramount's top echelon waiting for him at the studio conference table.

"Gentlemen," Coop addressed the assembled officials, "Gary Cooper is back — not a substitute, but the real thing."

"But, Gary," one of the executives implored, "those stories that we tried to replace you with Cary Grant are meaningless. Why, we never for a moment considered anyone for your place."

"No one's going to take my place," snapped Coop, surprising even himself with his boldness.

"Now let me tell you what I want in my new contract. First, I want more money. More than you've offered. Much more. . . ."

Several of the executives shifted uneasily in their chairs.

"Then I'd like a bigger say in what pictures I make and the number that I'll play in every year. I don't want to be coming down with jaundice and anemia because of overwork."

The Paramount biggies were ready now to call for the ulcer pills. Their star had come back from Africa strangely a tiger.

"And I want," Coop continued, "stories that are credible. They've got to fit me, my personality. The fans have a definite impression of me. They see me as an individual, and that's the way I've got to keep coming over to them. . . ."

Coop's uncompromising stand worked. All except for the money part; that remained at $2,500, but with provisions in a seven-year contract for periodic raises that would bring him up to $7,500 a week.

In the weeks ahead, the whole world seemed to smile on the big lanky cowhand from Montana. As one of the provisions of his eminently satisfying new contract, Coop got to play in Ernest Hemingway's *A Farewell to Arms,* costarring with the gifted Helen Hayes.

He also had occasion to see again the aspiring young actress whom he'd met back East, Veronica Balfe. Veronica had come to Hollywood, assertedly to pursue a movie career, but actually . . . well, let's continue with the facts.

Again, Gary and Veronica met at a party, and again, in the first moments of their encounter, there was an awkward silence between them. But Veronica soon sent the barriers tumbling by telling Coop of the impression he had made on her in *Morocco,* the picture he had appeared in with Marlene Dietrich. Veronica had been a student at the exclusive Bennett School for Girls, near Millbrook, N. Y., and she and several of her classmates had gone to see the film. She remembered Gary Cooper as the romantic hero.

Coop sensed that Veronica was attracted to him — and he had a feeling for Veronica. Coop's feeling could be explained in a four-letter word spelled l–o–v–e.

But what about the countess?

It was a delicate situation, yet it was ultimately solved — heartbreakingly for the countess, according to no less an authority than Elsa Maxwell.

Miss Maxwell by now had arrived in Los Angeles and had gone to stay at Gary's house in the Chevy Chase section of Beverly Hills, which was the abode he had rented from Greta Garbo. Miss Garbo might have dispossessed Coop had she known that he literally had loaded her walls with the trophies of his African safari.

"Those walls," said Miss Maxwell, "were just filled with heads of antelopes, lions, and leopard skins."

For six weeks, Elsa was a guest at Coop's house, all during the filming of Selznick's *Our Betters.*

"During my stay," Miss Maxwell related, "I met a galaxy of stars that would have answered any screenwriter's ambition — Clark Gable, Bob Hope, Cary Grant (whom Coop no longer feared), Carole Lombard, Helen Hayes, Fredric March, and many others.

"Gary, who was a silent, rather inarticulate man, under Dorothy's tutelage became a great host. Dorothy would come every morning to have breakfast with us. That she adored the handsome Cooper was evident; she was so honest and uninhibited that her emotions and actions were never restricted to conventional behavior — a child of nature, she showed her feelings without any reserve.

"I think Cooper returned her devotion in the beginning. But she was older, and Gary's romantic feelings mellowed to an affectionate friendship which I think must have hurt Dorothy more than she ever let on."

Any romantic feelings Coop may have had for the Countess di Frasso evidently paled quickly in the presence of Veronica Balfe. The countess realized that Gary had fallen for Veronica. It made her desperately unhappy, yet she tried to hang on.

Moreover, to make things worse for her, the countess was not only competing with Veronica for Coop's affections, but there was also another female to contend with — for Lupe Velez was still very much in the picture with Coop.

Hollywood gossip columnists, making the most of the stories of Coop's several female admirers, aroused a marked hostility in Veronica's uncle, Cedric Gibbons, who had promised her mother to keep an eye on Veronica while she was in Hollywood. Gibbons set a strict evening curfew on Veronica's dates with Coop.

Coop didn't mind much. He was too busy to care because he had plunged into the important business of making *Farewell to Arms.*

Helen Hayes, costarring with Gary, came to Hollywood with some apprehension about her leading man, for his reputation as a lady-killer had reached far and wide. His Riviera exploits with the Countess di Frasso and his earlier galavanting with leading ladies like Evelyn Brent, Clara Bow, and more recently Lupe Velez, made him seem a dangerous character in the eyes of a prim and proper young lady like Miss Hayes.

Coop was somewhat frightened of Miss Hayes because her stature in the theater was taller than that of any actress he had ever appeared with.

Director Frank Borzage, who met Coop and Miss Hayes in his office the first day they reported to work, had a horrendous time getting the two to warm up to each other.

"It was like two icebergs crossing off the Greenland coast," reported an assistant director who worked in Paramount at the time. "Borzage saw how thick the ice was and it didn't please him. His worst fear was that a thaw might not come. And to play the roles they had been assigned in Hemingway's great love story, they just had to warm up to one another.

"Frank figured out a way to solve the problem. He told them he wanted to shoot some publicity stills and sent Coop and Miss Hayes to their dressing rooms to put on their costumes. When they came out, he called to the grips to bring a couch. Then he had Coop and Miss Hayes lie down. Miss Hayes seemed reluctant, although she followed the director's instructions.

"Coop stretched his long frame obediently alongside Miss Hayes, but left a respectable distance between himself and the actress. Too respectable for a warm love scene.

"Frank cried out something like, 'Please, please, we are playing a love scene. Can't you people get closer?'

"They finally did and Borzage hurried over to the camera and peered through the ground glass. He shouted 'magnificent' and said he thought it would make a smashing picture if Coop and Miss Hayes could act out the picture on the couch.

"That brought a roar of laughter from Coop and Miss Hayes — and melted the ice. They played together wonderfully, although Borzage had one hell of a time figuring the camera angles to avoid the awkward pose of Coop, all six feet plus of him, towering over Miss Hayes, whose eyes could barely scan higher than Coop's third rib."

Coop and Helen Hayes worked together like a well-drilled team, and the great Hemingway story was faithfully transcribed from the pages of the book into a celluloid epic.

The reviews on the film were tremendous. With the possible exception of Mordaunt Hall, the New York *Times* movie critic, *A Farewell to Arms* was enthusiastically received, and movie audiences thrilled to the combination of

Broadway's First Lady in the arms of Gary Cooper.

Regina Crewe, the motion picture editor of the New York *Journal-American*, represented the majority viewpoint in the reviews:

"It's told with a feeling, a frankness, a depth, and a daring that marks a milestone in the production of motion pictures. It provides Gary Cooper, caparisoned in the fine, full horizon blue cape of this romantic wartime front with the finest, brightest Bersallieri plume that has ever decorated his histrionic helmet. It affords Miss Hayes an opportunity to eclipse her justly lauded former efforts, and it allows Adolphe Menjou to harness his chargers to an actor's chariot for another triumph.

"Motion pictures have been adolescent for a long, long time. Now, suddenly, overnight, they leap to full maturity and stalwart stature. *A Farewell to Arms* means greeting to a brighter, better day in the history of motion pictures."

With *A Farewell to Arms* completed, Gary Cooper resumed his courtship of Veronica Balfe with all the ardor of an Iowa schoolboy at his first sight of the beautiful new schoolmarm.

As it became increasingly clear that Gary was sincere in his relations with Veronica and not simply on a lark, even the avuncular hostility of Cedric Gibbons melted away, and they were allowed to spend more and more time alone. The Hollywood gossip columnists leaped anew at the chance to publicize the new "romance" and played it for all the mileage they could get. They got very little mileage, because Gary and Veronica soon learned her folks back East looked upon their daughter's romance with the cowpoke–playboy–actor with considerable disfavor.

Veronica had led a somewhat sheltered life under the guardianship of her stepfather, multimillionaire Paul

Shields, and she moved in the rarefied circles of the best of Eastern society. She had attended exclusive schools, had been a debutante, wintered on Park Avenue, summered at Southampton. She was a member in good standing of New York society, and the prospect of becoming emotionally entangled with a Montana-born cowboy was enough to chill some of that rich blue blood back home.

Mr. and Mrs. Shields were horrified that Veronica would fall for a Hollywood actor with a reputation as an unscrupulous rake who was always romantically linked with his leading ladies.

As it turned out, Coop's greatest ally in his battle to win the approval of the Shields was Cedric Gibbons.

Gibbons came to the rescue at the crucial moment when Veronica's mother was contemplating coming out to California to bring Veronica home. Gibbons grabbed the phone, called his sister in New York, and proceeded to pacify her with a reassuring buildup of her daughter's beau.

According to a Hollywood source, renowned for her eavesdropping capabilities, the conversation that ensued went like this:

"Why, do you know that Gary Cooper is the nicest, sweetest, shyest young man in all Hollywood?" she quoted Gibbons as having said. "He comes from one of the finest families in all the West — his father was a Supreme Court judge. Real American stock. And Gary is a college man. What more could you ask for? I tell you, sis, there's nobody better than Gary. Do you want Veronica to end up marrying a Yale or Harvard man?"

At any rate, whether those were the exact words or not, the fact remains that the famed art director was now solidly behind Gary Cooper.

But what of the Countess di Frasso and Lupe Velez? Would they give up without an elimination fight?

Elsa Maxwell provided the answer to what happened to the countess, relating the story from her unfailing memory of such epochal events.

Dorothy, according to Elsa, received an invitation from Veronica one day to come to lunch. Veronica, or Rocky, as she had been nicknamed by her classmates back in school, said she had something important for the countess. The countess showed up.

"It was a real frame-up," Dorothy told Elsa. "I went to the Mocambo at the appointed time to find not only Rocky but also Lupe Velez. I had given Gary some emerald studs and cuff links for his birthday.

"Rocky threw them across the table saying:

" 'Gary wanted you to have these back — he has no use for them now.'

"When Miss Velez said the same thing, I knew it was a frame-up. Somehow I became what I have never claimed to be in my life before — a lady.

"I would have liked to crack a plate over both their heads, but I walked out with a dignified bow to both these dames.

"But how unnecessary it was and how rude they were."

The countess had tears in her eyes as she spoke to Miss Maxwell.

"I loved Gary and was and always will be his friend," she said.

That's how the countess was eliminated from Gary's life.

Now for Lupe. Her downfall was less painful. She simply decided that she could not be tied down to a man. Her swan song was, "I must be free ... I will never have a boss. ..."

The road was clear for Gary and Veronica.

All that was left now was to name the date. Coop and Veronica decided on it, but the world, filled with rumors of the impending wedding, would not be told. So the newspapers and the columnists worked overtime on their hunches.

On November 6, 1933 — fully five weeks before they planned to say their I do's — a story flashed out of Hollywood reporting Gary Cooper and Sandra Shaw in Phoenix, Arizona, with actress Virginia Bruce and her husband, Jack Gilbert, on a hunting trip, but added that "friends hinted at a possible elopement."

Coop denied this in print the very next day.

"You can definitely quote me as saying Miss Shaw and I will not marry while here," he said.

On November 13, Sandra Shaw met the press in Hollywood and showed the fourth estaters her engagement ring, an impressive square-cut diamond. Smiling, the debutante-turned-actress, who had won the heart of the man all filmland was calling "Hollywood's most eligible bachelor," looked at the reporters and said:

"You'll have to get the date from Gary. He is spokesman."

Coop blushed. He said he wasn't certain of the date, but he allowed as how bachelorhood no longer appealed to him.

"Sandra is the ideal girl for me," he told the newsmen. "She can ride, shoot, and do all the things I like to do."

There was just one big question that still hung over the projected wedding — whether Veronica's mother and stepfather would have any final objections. The problem never came up. On November 28, Veronica's mother gave an engagement party in her sumptuous Park Avenue home.

Early arrivals thought the engagement party was going to be a wedding ceremony, judging by the decorations. Lilies were stacked in profusion in the living room, and the fireplace was hidden behind a forest of flowers that resembled an altar.

Veronica made her grand entrance in a silver lamé dress with a red velvet collar, while Gary appeared in tails. Both battled their way through well-wishers to greet Mrs. Shields, who was waiting with a broad, approving smile and a warm welcoming kiss for her daughter and future son-in-law.

Among the guests were Helen Hayes and her playwright husband, Charles MacArthur, Elsa Maxwell, composer Cole Porter, and dozens of other well-known celebrities.

A week later, Coop was interviewed by a New York reporter who got Gary to confide:

"My ideal woman is one who will stay at home and make a home for her husband. When Veronica Balfe and I are married, I think she will give up her film career."

Veronica Balfe gave up her movie career at 2 P.M., December 15, 1933. She was united in marriage to Gary Cooper in her mother's Park Avenue home by the Reverend George A. Trowbridge, rector of All Angels Church.

Coop, blushing, fidgeting, gulping nervously, showed up for the wedding in a brown-and-tan-checked double-breasted suit, with blue-and-red tie and English oxfords, and a white carnation in his lapel. He towered over the small gathering in the family drawing room with its white rugs, white curtains, white fireplace, and bowls of white flowers.

The bride wore a gray crepe-and-satin dress, gray corduroy hat, halo style, gray corduroy coat with sables, and brown suede pumps. She carried a small bouquet of lilies of the valley. She didn't appear half as nervous as the bridegroom.

Only four persons witnessed the ceremony: Mr. and Mrs. Paul Shields, the bride's mother and stepfather; her stepsister, Barbara Shields; and Jack Moss, Gary's secretary. For the record, Gary's secretary accompanied his boss and bride aboard the Twentieth Century Limited on their honeymoon to Phoenix, Arizona.

In Phoenix, Gary and Veronica found his parents waiting. They had come east from California to meet the bride. They were delighted with their son's wife and at once took to Veronica as their own daughter.

"She's radiant, beautiful, charming, and so intelligent," Mrs. Cooper enthused. Gary's mother was speaking for most of the people who had ever met Veronica.

His wife's influence on Gary Cooper was almost immediate. Marriage to Veronica Balfe gave Coop a sudden sense of responsibility which he had never exhibited before.

In his own story in the *Saturday Evening Post*, Coop said:

"If Veronica seemed delighted with being rescued from acting, work she didn't enjoy, I was equally delighted to be rescued from my career as a playboy. Both of us were so pleased to settle down that we did it wholesale."

Gary gave up his bachelor quarters, which Louella Parsons has probably described most accurately — "a place that somewhat resembled a stuffed animal compound." The walls were decorated with all sorts of heads of wild animals Gary had shot in Africa, and the floors were literally blanketed with skins. The center of attraction — over the fireplace — was a huge moose head.

Gary and his bride bought a house they fell in love with, an "Early Iowa Barn" as Coop called it, and settled down on its ten acres of land. The place had orange and lemon groves behind the house, and Coop even bought a tractor with the good intention of emulating some of the other Hollywood screen notables who tilled their own soil, raised their own crops, and kept a menagerie of livestock.

But the burden of picture making kept Coop occupied full time at the studio. Before long he had to give up the idea of being Farmer Cooper. They sold out and built a Bermuda-style low-lying whitewashed ranch house which sprawled over the green hills of Brentwood. It was an elegant atmosphere, yet exceedingly simple. It was here that Gary and Rocky found true contentment.

More and more Gary Cooper was beginning to pull his weight at the box office. More and more exhibitors shouted to the studio, "Give us Gary Cooper pictures," and they didn't much care what the pictures were about, or who else was in them, or how much artistic quality might have seeped into the films. Their only concern seemed to be with their marquees — they wanted Gary Cooper up there.

Coop met the challenge by plunging into film after film as quickly as the studio could produce the script and sign up the cast; he was well on his way to becoming the motion picture industry's biggest and most dependable attraction.

CHAPTER FOURTEEN

Gary's Galaxy Gets a $482,821 Gold Lining

Marriage and his newly settled life seemed to add a fresh and deeper dimension to Gary Cooper. Maturity came, and with it, confidence — confidence in himself, both as a man and as an actor. He began to develop powerful new acting techniques that brought him, with each succeeding picture, ever-widening popularity and increasingly consistent critical acclaim.

His first picture after returning to work was *Operator 13*, a comedy–drama of Civil War days which teamed him with the incomparably beautiful Marion Davies. It was a spectacularly staged presentation about a young girl torn between love and duty, confronted with the problem of choosing between the man and the cause she dearly loves. Miss Davies appeared as an entertainer recruited into the ranks of Union spies and assigned to get one dashing Confederate captain, Gary Cooper. His performance was described by reviewers as "stirring and unforgettable."

There was one factor of historic significance that figured

in Coop's appearance in *Operator 13*. It marked the second time in his movie career that he had strayed from Paramount to make a film for another studio. Of his 35 major movies, Cooper had starred in 33 for Paramount and in one, *Lilac Time*, for First National. Making *Operator 13* for Metro-Goldwyn-Mayer did not signal the end of Cooper's relationship with Paramount. Actually he was still working under the fabulous new Paramount contract negotiated on his return from his overseas adventures, and he was now making $3,000 a week. His role for MGM was sanctioned by his studio, which had put Gary on a "loan-out" to the rival studio.

His success in *Operator 13* was quickly followed by *Now and Forever*, back at Paramount again, in which he was costarred with the vivacious Carole Lombard and the baby Bernhardt of the day, Shirley Temple. The script didn't exactly shortchange Coop's or Carole's acting talents; nevertheless, it wasn't difficult to see that the place of honor in the film was reserved for the five-year-old dimpled darling, whose every gleeful gurgle would make moviegoers sigh ecstatically.

"I didn't mind having the scenes stolen from under my nose," Coop laughed when he talked about his encounter with his knee-high adversary for film honors. "I was beginning to be accused by lots of folks in Hollywood of stealing scenes, so maybe it was a good thing for me to be the victim for a change."

There was a steadfastness about Coop, and a marked degrce of good sportsmanship. And as the graph of his career and his work continued upward, Coop invested certain ingredients which could spell only success into his career and his work — the ingredients of high principle, hard work, self-control, and great good humor.

In 1935, Coop reached another plateau in the cinema

firmament, when Paramount picked him for the lead in *Lives of a Bengal Lancer.* This was to be a big picture with lavish sets, spectacular scenes, and a huge cast, including such stars as Franchot Tone, Richard Cromwell, Sir Guy Standing, Kathleen Burke, C. Aubrey Smith, and Akim Tamiroff.

His appearance in this movie also meant Coop's first separation from his bride; the entire troop had to camp out for a month on a special 500-acre ranch location that was to be the "Khyber Pass" in the film. While it did not in the least strain their marriage, the separation nevertheless made both Gary and Veronica realize that his film career would put demands on their marriage that required patience and understanding.

"We were both willing to sacrifice," Coop said. "Once you start working on a picture, especially something as demanding of your time and energy as *Lives of a Bengal Lancer,* you've got to fully devote yourself to the assignment. What a man needs most then is an understanding wife. Veronica was all that — and more.

"Working day and night on a picture is a terrific strain not only for the guy who does it, but his wife. If Rocky wasn't an understanding person, I don't know what might have happened during that month I spent sweating my way through *Lancer.*"

And at home, that strain Coop talked about was apparent in Rocky. She waited for Coop to return after *Lancer,* to pick up the threads of their home life in the glow of the picture's big success.

Coop enjoyed the glory that came with it, and also the fact that he was being offered a lot of leeway in his selection of scripts.

After *Lancer,* the starring roles came one on top of the

other — *Her Wedding Night, Peter Ibbetson, Desire, The General Died at Dawn.* And with each film, one actor after another, and actresses too, invariably discovered that in playing with Coop they had to content themselves with the inevitable — that Gary Cooper was always the star of the picture.

And at home, Rocky Cooper had to face the inevitable too. Gary had to be the star there also.

"As a big star," Rocky recalled for Sidney Fields, author of the column, "Only Human," then in the New York *Mirror*, "he had to be number one, as any wife married to one can tell you. A woman married to a star has to get used to the fact that everyone looks at him first, especially women, and the wife gets the second look — if that."

This apparently pained Veronica, who had been used to gathering the stares back in her social world in the East. But she couldn't fight it.

"Coop told me fights always upset him and we just weren't going to have any. He laid down the law and I listened. You have to, if you don't want to lose your husband."

Nevertheless, Rocky admitted that, despite the background role she apparently felt she was playing, she actually had the idea she was a real big wheel. But her mother advised her:

"Don't ride on your husband's coattails. Develop your own personality."

To Rocky this was a huge order. It meant she would have to be a little wheel, especially in the presence of other women who'd always be eyeing her man wherever they went.

"That was the toughest adjustment to make," Rocky admitted. "I just learned not to look at the other women."

The formula worked well for Rocky — and for Coop.

As Gary continued to hold the upper hand both at home and at the studio, his fame mounted and his assignments became even more choice.

After *The General Died at Dawn*, Columbia Studios negotiated with Paramount for a loan of its star for a satiric and delightful film it was planning to make under the direction of Frank Capra. It was with no reluctance at all that Coop agreed to work under Capra at Columbia, for the director was fresh from his triumphant Academy Award effort of the previous year, *It Happened One Night*, costarring Claudette Colbert and Clark Gable.

"Working for Capra," Coop said, "meant that I would have one of the very best directors in the business and I would be getting an excellent opportunity to try out what I always wanted to do on a large scale — subdued comedy."

.The name of the picture was *Mr. Deeds Goes to Town*, and in stepping into the shoes of the taciturn Longfellow Deeds of Clarence Buddington Kelland's story, Coop's flair for subdued comedy enabled him to make the hero's peregrinations a series of highly entertaining adventures.

The film, which costarred Jean Arthur as Babe Bennett, was a rousing success. Coop was the screen's man of the hour and critics everywhere hailed him as one of the greats of Hollywood.

Mr. Deeds, even in the years to come, remained one of Coop's favorites on the lengthy list of films he was to make. "It was the most enjoyable I ever made," he said. "I liked Mr. Deeds. Heck of a good fellow. Wish I could meet him somewhere."

It was not unusual now for different Gary Cooper films

to play simultaneously in one city in competition with each other. In 1936, for example, Coop's *Desire* opened for its first run in the New York Paramount, and a few days later, just blocks away at Rockefeller Center, the same huge crowds storming the Paramount came piling into Radio City Music Hall to catch Gary in *Mr. Deeds Goes to Town.*

But all work and no play was not Coop's aim in life, and he wasn't going to let any studio put him on the day–night film-making kick which had brought on jaundice and anemia a few years before. Now that he had achieved stature that few film stars enjoyed, Coop could begin to be more choosy about the pictures he played in — and the number of films he made.

He wanted more time to relax, to enjoy the life that he and Rocky wanted to live.

And their life together took on fuller and more joyous meaning on September 15, 1937.

The birth of their daughter, given the full name of Maria Veronica Balfe Cooper, brought this happy statement from Gary Cooper:

"I'm real proud in having a daughter. Mighty proud. A girl's got it all over a boy — and is a lot prettier."

Coop announced that as soon as Maria was old enough to ski, he and Rocky would take her up to Sun Valley, a resort that was fast becoming a regular hideaway for Gary and his wife whenever there was a break between pictures.

A deep friendship that had developed between Gary and Ernest Hemingway after *A Farewell to Arms* continued to flourish with the years. Coop and Rocky often joined Hemingway and his wife on hunting trips or bird shoots.

"I do not hunt," Rocky often remarked, "but I go along. I am a good skeet shot, but I will not kill an animal."

Coop had taught Rocky to shoot, by firing at tin cans.

In time she became a crack shot and in 1939 was so proficient she won the California Women's Skeetshooting Championship.

Gary and Veronica also spent time with Neddie and Gloria McLean on their Denver ranch, where Coop had numerous chances to show Rocky what real ranch life was like.

Gary would throw himself over a saddle and chase a steer over the corrals while Rocky watched from a distance.

"No one would believe you could punish yourself this way," she told Gary once after he dismounted, dust covering his perspiring face. "You really love this life, don't you?"

"I sure do. Making pictures is all right, but making a roundup beats making pictures anytime."

For the most part, Gary's and Rocky's life of leisure in those first years of their marriage was spent in activities such as hunting, swimming, golfing, and tennis. Rocky was a natural athlete, and with her as a coach, Coop began catching up on some of the sports he had missed all his life.

Meanwhile, Coop was continuing to establish his image on celluloid and the nation's theater screens with unparalleled success. He seemed to concentrate on projecting himself as the cowboy hero, despite his versatility in the many roles he played. He preserved the image by making one Western between every two or three films with contemporary settings, even if it meant being repetitive, even if it meant making a bad film.

He also was a man of great willpower, and proved it to everyone's satisfaction in 1938 when David O. Selznick offered him the prized role of Rhett Butler in *Gone with the Wind.* Coop rejected it. He did not see himself as quite that dashing.

His reason, he told an interviewer once, was that he wanted to retain his hold on the image he had projected on his public — a man who played roles that fit his personality.

"When I saw the way Clark Gable played the role," Coop told his interviewer, "I knew I had made the right decision. It was a very tempting offer. I'm glad I didn't take it."

Coop continued to film only pictures he was convinced didn't conflict with his fans' concept of him, and the pictures justified his efforts to carry that determination through.

After *Souls at Sea*, in which he was starred with George Raft and Frances Dee in a thrilling adventure of the high seas, Coop's next two pictures were made for Sam Goldwyn, the producer who had given him his first real part back in 1925 in *The Winning of Barbara Worth*. Goldwyn borrowed Coop for two big productions, *The Adventures of Marco Polo* and *The Cowboy and the Lady*. By making these pictures big, lavish screen spectacles, Goldwyn bid fair to outdo Cecil B. DeMille who had a virtual monopoly on that sort of extravaganza.

From Goldwyn, Coop went back to Paramount to do *Bluebeard's Eighth Wife*, in which he shared acting honors with Claudette Colbert once again, and Edward Everett Horton and David Niven. The film showed Gary as an oft-married millionaire who pursues Claudette, hoping to make her wife number eight. Many reviewers found it hard to believe that a character who had seven wives could be just a small boy at heart — which was Coop's principal charm.

Paramount next cast Coop in a remake of *Beau Geste*, which had first starred Ronald Colman back in 1926. Shrewdly enough, director William Wellman did not attempt to revamp the story for his 13-years-later audience. He stuck close to the old script and came up with a hit, something other directors had not generally been able to achieve on remakes, because invariably they would try new techniques and new methods of telling the story. Again Coop had a first-class list of costars — Ray Milland, Robert Preston, Brian Donlevy, Susan Hayward, J. Carroll Naish, and Broderick Crawford.

Returning once more to the image his public knew best, the strong silent hero of the cactus country, Coop starred in *The Westerner* — again for Samuel Goldwyn. Although Gary played the title role in the film, the story centered mostly on Walter Brennan, who impersonated the legendary whiskered, whisky-sopped, ruthless "Judge" Roy Bean, self-appointed "Law West of the Pecos" and fervent admirer from afar of Lily Langtry. Coop had ample warning after looking over the script and told himself this picture was not for him.

"I couldn't figure for the life of me why they needed me for this picture," Coop related. "I had a very minor part. It didn't require any special effort. All the character I played had to do was exchange a few shots with the judge in the dramatic moment of the picture. For that, I asked myself, why do they need Gary Cooper?"

Outspoken as he always was, Coop decided to convey his feelings to director William Wyler.

"You may not have the greatest part in the picture," Wyler told Coop," but that's not the way I see it. My idea is how well can you play the role you have? I think you'll look great in it."

Coop took the part, but resentfully. That brought an admonition from Wyler, who told Gary:

"You're not being a good sport about this. If you have

any feeling for this business of acting you'll put yourself into the role and play it for everything it's worth."

Wyler had made Coop feel like a heel. He brooded several days, then went to the director.

"Bill, I've thought over what you said. I believe you're right. I'll give my part everything I've got regardless of its size. I'm sorry I blew up."

Coop's part was not of the usual length to which his fans had been accustomed. But he lost no ground in popularity. His public loved him, even if Walter Brennan did hold the spotlight.

Then came another picture for Paramount, *Northwest Mounted Police*, which teamed Coop with a star-studded cast including Madeleine Carroll, Paulette Goddard, Preston Foster, Robert Preston, and George Bancroft. It was a big picture, and understandably so, since Cecil B. DeMille produced and directed it. Bosley Crowther, the New York *Times* critic, raved about it as a spectacular film. He found some fault with many of the actors, but about the star, Crowther wrote: "Only Mr. Cooper preserves his· cool, dry, congenial personality. He is himself, even in a DeMille film.

DeMille once was asked how he liked working with Coop.

"Great," he replied. "The thing about Gary Cooper that has impressed me most is his amazing alertness. From the time we made our first picture I have realized that he never misses a thing that goes on before the camera.

"People who see Cooper lounging off camera don't know what's going on behind those half-closed eyes. But I know he's developing the business and characterization that bring naturalness and humanness to his parts in my pictures.

"While Gary leans against a prop, chewing a match or a straw, he is checking every detail of setup and dialogue; noticing just how his stand-in is being lighted and almost invariably working out a suggestion to improve a camera angle or a bit of business."

Following his effort for DeMille, Coop went into *Meet John Doe*, and in this one Coop achieved some of his finest notices for his portrayal of the great American yap — the backbone of this country, the sturdiest citizen there is — shy, bewildered, nonaggressive, but a veritable tiger when aroused. Barbara Stanwyck, Walter Brennan, and Edward Arnold held down the other top roles in the film that carried an inspiring lesson on Americanism at a time when the world was being darkened with frightening swiftness by the spreading clouds of war.

After the premiere, Gary and Veronica went to Ciro's for a celebration. Everyone came over to the table to congratulate Coop for his excellent portrayal. One of those who trotted up was William Holden, a Cooper fan from way back. Holden was extravagant in his praise of Gary, perhaps too much so in his open admiration.

One thing that irked Coop was effusive praise, and he often reverted to slapping down a flatterer with salty cowhand language. In this instance, however, Coop wanted to spare Holden's feelings so he tried to shift the credit over to the director.

"Frank Capra did a fine job of it, didn't he?" Coop asked.

But Holden kept showering praise on him, so Coop finally blurted:

"Now, Bill, you cut the bullshit."

Veronica, aghast, tugged frantically at Coop's coatsleeve.

"Beg pardon, Bill," said Coop, grinning. "Meant to say 'you cut out the baloney.'"

His venture to Ciro's was one of Coop's rare nights out, for he and Veronica went nightclubbing infrequently. Coop just didn't go for the social life. Once, after another night out, the gang at the studio ribbed him with innocent questions: "Have a good time last night, Coop?" Gary kept silent for several moments. Finally, he glimpsed his hecklers with narrowed eyes and a wry grin.

"Sure were a lot of people there who *thought* they were havin' themselves a good time!"

In the midst of his great series of successes, Gary Cooper fans and the nation as a whole were almost floored by a story that came out of Washington on August 2, 1940, announcing:

"Gary Cooper topped all the nation's wage earners in 1939, and nosed out the business machine and soap manufacturers who previously had held the distinction of highest-paid Americans. Cooper rolled up a total paycheck for the year of $482,821, Treasury Secretary Morgenthau disclosed tonight.

"He was followed by Thomas J. Watson, head of International Business Machines — an 'ex-champ' — who earned $420,299; F. A. Countway of Lever Bros., soap manufacturers, $383,201; General Motors ex-chief William S. Knudsen, now defense director, $372,366, and James Cagney, $368,333."

To Hollywood, the story meant one thing — a lot of people were seeing Gary Cooper's pictures. To Coop, who had become the first movie actor to lead the list of income earners in the United States, it meant:

"The public must look on me as a composite of all the characters I've played ... I must mean a lot of things to different people. I've played, God knows, every conceivable role — a French Foreign Legionnaire, a cowboy, a mountie, a Jazz Age gigolo, and many more types. I guess maybe it's that composite the public likes."

What did this composite really look like?

Who was he?

And how could Gary Cooper be responsible for him?

"An actor's got plenty of time between appearances before camera to study himself," Coop said in a moment of self-critical analysis. "Although there's lots to be done at the studio, like spending time dressing and putting on makeup, besides studying script and acting, there are also hours of free time in between. I find that to preserve the mood of the character I'm playing I've got no choice but to think. And when I'm not thinking, I sleep."

Pretty much in line with what DeMille — and many other directors — said.

Coop always struggled to fulfill his responsibility to the moviegoing public, of making certain to his complete satisfaction that every character in a film was written to his unique specifications so that his image was never distorted. In a word, stories had to fit his personality.

The first great struggle to meet his responsibility to his public came one day early in 1941 when producer Hal Wallis showed Coop a script called *Sergeant York*, based on the real-life story of the magnificent hero of World War I who achieved his niche in history by capturing an entire German machine-gun battalion of 132 men in the Argonne Forest singlehandedly.

Coop looked over the script. Some quick thoughts passed through his mind. To his way of thinking, in screen biographies dealing with historical personages, a change in the character's role could be accomplished by the studio without seriously damaging either the reputation or image of the person. But York was a great hero who was still alive and whose legendary feats in war were more dramatic than any fictional achievements, and Coop felt he could not possibly project himself into the part with the impact needed to do complete justice to the real-life hero.

York himself came to tell Coop he was his own choice for the role. But Coop still felt he couldn't handle it.

Cooper told Wallis his feelings.

"York's just too big for me to handle," Coop said. "He covered too much ground."

So far as Gary Cooper was concerned, the role of *Sergeant York* was not for him.

The Road to Glory—
Sergeant York

The dark clouds that had blanketed Europe in the cata-
clysm of World War II were blowing ominously and relentlessly toward America's shores in early 1941, and the
country was in the midst of mobilization for the day when
it would inevitably have to join the conflict.

Already, Hollywood's film makers were engaged in
turning out movies with patriotic themes. The film capital's
top stars were in heavy demand to fill the roles in the new
production program.

But Gary Cooper wanted no part of the great story
Hollywood was prepared to tell about the nation's most
celebrated war hero — Sergeant Alvin York. His rejection
of the role offered by Hal Wallis had the ring of finality
about it, and Coop felt he would not hear about it again.

After visiting Southampton on Long Island with
Rocky's parents, Coop and his wife came into New York
City and took a hotel suite for a few days to make the
rounds of the new Broadway shows. One afternoon Gary

came downstairs to the lobby to buy a newspaper. He ran into Jesse L. Lasky, the producer.

"What in tarnation you doin' in this part of the country?" Coop asked.

"I'm still looking for Sergeant York," Lasky smiled.

"Wouldn't want to change your mind?"

Lasky was casual about it, but serious. He had already learned from his associate, Hal Wallis, how Coop felt about playing the lead in *Sergeant York*. But Lasky had decided to make his own bid for Gary's services. In Lasky's mind, no one but Gary Cooper would do.

The story of the great war hero had been Lasky's personal venture for nearly 22 years, since the day the real Alvin C. York had been escorted up New York's Fifth Avenue in the Armistice Day Parade of 1919. One of the people who stood in the cheering crowd was Jesse Lasky, then production head of the Famous Players Lasky Studio. Lasky made up his mind then that someday he would produce a motion picture based on Sergeant York's story.

York had been a zealous churchgoer, and, because of his deep religious conviction that killing under any circumstances was a sin against God, he was a conscientious objector. But he underwent a remarkable change as he watched war in all its horror, and on October 6, 1918, in the Argonne Forest, York wiped out a sector of German machine-gun nests, killing 25 Germans and capturing 132 — the biggest one-man catch in all recorded military history.

Lasky was not the only Hollywood film maker who saw the significance of York's story as World War II approached. The Tennessean had been deluged with dozens of offers and could have made a potful of money had he accepted any of them. But he preferred his peaceful backwoods life to the glare of the Hollywood spotlight, and when York went home the offers stopped.

In the years that followed, Lasky's production affiliations changed. At the brink of World War II he was an independent producer, and now he decided to go all out for York's story. After several telegrams, Lasky went personally to see Sergeant York in the Valley of the Three Forks of the Wolf, where he lived with his family.

York finally agreed to allow his story to be made into a film but stipulated all the proceeds accruing to him from the picture must be turned over to the various religious organizations in which he was deeply interested. It was so agreed.

During the negotiations, York stressed to Lasky that his personal choice for the title role was Gary Cooper. Later, York himself got in touch with Coop and told him so.

With Lasky and York both pleading, Coop found good reason to stop and reflect.

"I asked myself what do I have to do to make York come alive as the great hero he was," Coop said. "I knew I had to understand the sergeant intimately — know his thinking, his motivations, his principles. There was only one way to find those things out. Visit him and talk with him."

So Coop visited the old soldier in his beloved Tennessee mountains. There, in those surroundings, Coop saw the quiet faith and philosophy of the peaceful Sergeant York. Gary was deeply impressed — York didn't smoke, didn't drink, didn't swear.

Coop had tried to give up smoking himself and hadn't been able to. "That characteristic was enough to applaud," Coop remarked.

But above all, Coop recalled, he was impressed with the way York lived in peace with himself and the world and believed all men had the same right.

Coop spoke at length with America's great hero and

learned from him how his principles had been altered by the aggressive acts of foreign countries, which forced York to take up arms. He had fought because he wanted to preserve his country's freedom, a right that had been endowed to man by God.

After his meeting with York, Coop was convinced he could do justice to York's story.

The clouds of war swirled ever closer to American shores, and Gary knew that the dilemma that once faced York would be facing other Americans now.

"I knew I would put everything I had into it," Coop said. "I didn't want to do anything that might tarnish a national idol."

If he had fears about his ability, there were those who felt confident that all would be well.

Telegrams came to Coop from men in high places, including Secretary of State Cordell Hull, who wired: I KNOW YOU WILL DO FULL JUSTICE TO THE LIFE AND ACHIEVEMENTS OF A MOST REMARKABLE PERSON.

General John J. Pershing, who had called York "the greatest civilian soldier," also wired Coop: WISH YOU EVERY SUCCESS IN YOUR PORTRAYAL OF THIS FINE SOLDIER OF THE WORLD WAR.

The film, directed by Howard Hawks, was completely factual, and Sergeant York had so much confidence in the studio that he left everything in the hands of Lasky and Wallis. During his stay in Hollywood, York concerned himself more with Coop as a friend than as an actor. At the studio he would sit for hours talking with Gary about guns. When he had returned home, York sent Coop a 125-year-old muzzle-loading rifle which the sergeant had first used to train his sights.

During filming, Coop also spent considerable time firing on the range which had been set up near the studio. Coop, of course, was a crack marksman. His companion on these outings was Hawks, also an expert on the trigger.

One thing annoyed Coop in making *Sergeant York*. He didn't beef about it, but it embarrassed him — the fact that his leading lady, Joan Leslie, was so young, only sixteen.

The first day they met on the set, Joan was wearing a gingham dress and flat-heeled shoes. She looked about twelve years old. Someone brought Joan over and introduced her.

"Coop, here's your wife," Gary was told.

Coop looked, blushed, then gulped.

"I can see," Gary smiled, "how I'm gonna really feel like a hillbilly with a child bride."

Coop never could quite get accustomed to the idea of playing lover and husband to Miss Leslie. However, the public did.

Sergeant York had its world premiere in New York's Astor Theater on Broadway on the night of July 2, 1941. York himself was brought to the opening and given a rousing, bugle-blaring reception. The film was a smash hit. Reviewers went wild over it.

"*Sergeant York*, as it has come from under the wise and loving hand of director Howard Hawks," wrote Kate Cameron in the New York *Daily News*, "is not only one of the finest pictures of this year, but one of the greatest ever made in Hollywood."

Rose Pelswick, movie critic for the New York *Journal-American*, opened her review by saying America could use a few more pictures like *Sergeant York*, then went on to call it "thrilling drama" and to praise Gary Cooper for "superb acting."

"That part of York," Miss Pelswick wrote, "was made to order for the lean and lanky Cooper — one of the best pictures of this year or any year."

High praise was also heaped on the other stars, particularly Walter Brennan who played Pastor Rosier Pile, Joan Leslie who portrayed Gracie Williams, York's wife, and George Tobias as Pusher Rose.

The reaction to *Sergeant York* was in many ways unprecedented. Patriotic groups the country over lauded Coop for his role. The Veterans of Foreign Wars presented Gary with their Distinguished Citizenship Medal in recognition of his work in the film.

Coop's performance was officially recognized by the Academy of Motion Pictures and Sciences, which voted him the best actor of 1941 for his portrayal of Sergeant York.

It was fitting tribute to Gary Cooper, who had now made his public suddenly aware that the quiet cowboy who mirrored the legendary American hero of the Western ranges was a far better actor than most people ever bothered to suspect. The road that Coop had traveled from that long-ago day of 1925 when he galloped his stallion into the fence in moviedom's first do-it-yourself screen test, to the year 1941 when he achieved the honor of an "Oscar," was a rugged and perilous one. But Coop had traveled it with determination and certainty of purpose and had made good in one of the most competitive businesses in the world.

Coop accepted his award with humility and gratitude.

"It wasn't Gary Cooper who won this award," he said, "it was Sergeant York — because to the best of my ability I tried to be Sergeant York."

A few months after *Sergeant York* made its debut, war came to the United States and Hollywood mobilized for the effort. Many actors enlisted, others were drafted into the armed forces. Still others wanted to join up but couldn't because of physical impairments. Gary Cooper was one of the latter. That accident in Harvey Markham's Model T Ford rendered him 4-F.

The sequel to the accident came one day when Gary's hip began to act up and the studio sent him to the hospital for X-rays.

After a day of intensive examinations, the bone specialist came into Gary's room with an X-ray plate and pointed to a white line passing through Coop's hip.

During all those years Coop had been walking around with a broken hip!

The doctor was astounded when he learned that Gary's treatment was horseback riding rather than traction and complete rest.

In the years that followed, Coop often remarked how differently things might have turned out for him had he not gone off to his dad's ranch to take the long walks and learn to ride as he did — with an aching hip.

"Maybe it was the best advice that doctor gave me," Coop said. "Where would I have been if it hadn't happened? Here I can stand now and say a broken hip never did anyone any harm — look at me, for example."

Of course, it did prevent Coop from enlisting. This was the second time he had been thwarted in his efforts to serve his country in war. During World War I, he had watched his brother go off but he himself had been too young. Now he wasn't fit. But he was fit to carry on in his chosen profession and to inspire the nation with his screen performances.

The inspiration that *Sergeant York*, as played by Gary Cooper, had given the nation at a perilous time in its history could never be measured with a yardstick. The benefits sunk deep in the hearts and souls of men and gave them new spirit and courage to do their utmost for their country.

Of all the millions who felt a certain something when they viewed *Sergeant York*, no one could have matched the feelings of one aging soldier, placed on a hallowed pedestal by a grateful nation — Sergeant Alvin C. York himself.

"It was superb . . . perfect," he said, tears in his eyes.

The picture also touched another gray-haired gentleman, out on the Coast. It was former Montana Supreme Court Justice Cooper, Gary's dad, living with his wife in retirement in Hollywood. The elder Cooper had long since settled the estate case that had brought him West — but he had also settled into his own law offices in Hollywood. By 1941 he was retired and passed his time with friends, just chatting. Gary's mother spent much of her time engaged in charitable social work.

Their greatest enjoyment, however, was watching their son achieve increasing success, fame, and fortune in the movies.

And the movies just kept coming.

After his triumph in *Sergeant York*, Coop was grabbed by Sam Goldwyn for a delightful comedy called *Ball of Fire*, in which he was costarred with Barbara Stanwyck. Coop had the role of a literal-minded encyclopedist working on an analysis of current American slang. Barbara becomes his most fruitful source of slang terms, which is understandable when you consider that she plays a stripteaser, named Sugarbush O'Shea.

Bosley Crowther, in his review in the *Times*, praised the screen play and said that Coop was really "Mr. Deeds with a lot of book learning." Then he added that Gary's acting was a "homespun performance such as only he can give." Borrowing from the lingo of the day, Crowther described Barbara Stanwyck as "plenty of yum-yum (meaning scorchy) in her worldly temptress role."

Goldwyn quickly latched onto Coop for his next production, *The Pride of the Yankees*, the life story of the late Lou Gehrig, one of the greatest ballplayers of all time.

Goldwyn almost regretted his choice of Coop for Gehrig's role because, to the producer's and all Hollywood's complete astonishment, they learned that Gary had never played the national pastime in his whole life.

Actually Coop hadn't even been in the running for the part — at the outset. Four baseball fanatics named Eddie Albert, William Gargan, Dennis Morgan, and George Tobias had offered to play in the film just for the glory, or so the story goes. An equally frenetic fan named William Wellman offered to direct just for the fun of it, too.

Each of the four volunteers was a worthy candidate. Each bore a certain physical resemblance to the late Iron Man of the Yankees. But Sam Goldwyn struck them out because the producer was looking for a star with just the right qualities for the role.

Gary Cooper was such a man.

And even though Gary did not look like Lou Gehrig in face or build, Mrs. Lou Gehrig, the widow, was deeply impressed with Coop's qualities which were akin to her beloved husband's — modesty, sincerity, and capability. She endorsed Gary at once.

But when Goldwyn learned Coop, typical American though he was, couldn't play baseball — well, it was either un-Americanism or fantasy. Goldwyn couldn't believe it. But the truth of the matter was that Coop had never had a chance to learn the game. He had gone to school in England where the sport is either rugby or cricket. Baseball wasn't British.

To prepare Coop for the Lou Gehrig role, Christy Walsh, who had taught Gehrig and Babe Ruth among others, was retained to give Gary technical aid. In addition,

Babe Herman, the famous Brooklyn Dodgers outfielder who frequently caught fly balls with his skull, and Lefty O'Doul, ex-National League batting champion and discoverer of the DiMaggios — Joe, Vince, and Dominic — also were brought to Hollywood to help prepare Coop and offer advice in the making of the picture.

O'Doul was to teach Coop to look like a ballplayer, not necessarily to be one.

"I'll either make Coop look like a first baseman," O'Doul said, "or I'll break his leg."

One of the technical difficulties that plagued Goldwyn in the production was that Gary was right-handed. Gehrig had been a southpaw. But the problem was solved happily. The letters and numbers on Gary's uniform were reversed, the film was processed with the back side to the front — and Coop came up a left-hander in the picture.

Coop's big moment did not come during the making of the picture, but some months later. By that time he had kissed Rocky and his daughter Maria goodbye and gone off with a USO troupe of wartime entertainers to play for the boys in the South Pacific. Coop worked long and hard on that trip; he got to know the same mud and rain, inadequate shelter and rations as the soldiers, marines, and sailors stationed there.

At Port Moresby in New Guinea, one of the first stops on the tour, 10,000 soldiers sat in a drenching downpour and shouted to Coop to recite Lou Gehrig's farewell speech to the Yankees, as he had done in *Pride of the Yankees*. According to a story sent out by International News Service, Coop didn't remember the speech as well as he wanted to, so he went off to the side to jot it down on paper. Then he came back and announced, "All right, fellas, I've got it. ..." Then he read it, but not once, reported INS, did Coop have to refer to the script. It went like this, with all the emotional tug that Gehrig himself had imparted that day in Yankee Stadium when he recited it before 70,000 fans:

"I've been walking on ballfields for sixteen years, and I've never received anything but kindness and encouragement from you fans. I've had the great honor to have played with these great veteran ballplayers on my left — Murderers' Row — our championship team of 1927. I've had the further honor of living with and playing with these men on my right — the Bronx Bombers — the Yankees of today.

"I have been given fame and undeserved praise by the boys up there behind the wire in the press box — my friends — the sportswriters. I've worked under the two greatest managers of all time — Miller Huggins and Joe McCarthy.

"I have a mother and father who fought to give me health and a solid background in my youth. I have a wife — a companion for life — who has shown me more courage than I ever knew.

"People all say that I've had a bad break, but — today — today I consider myself the luckiest man on the face of the earth."

That was all. They were the words of a courageous American, a hero of the national pastime, whose life had only a short while to go, and everyone knew it.

Coop was called on again and again to recite Gehrig's farewell speech wherever he went on his 20,000-mile USO tour of Pacific bases.

And in the utter silence that would fall over audiences, in those moments it took to utter Gehrig's memorable farewell, Coop would be the personification of Lou Gehrig to those who watched and heard him.

When Coop returned to the States he went off on USO

tours of bases and hospitals all over the country. At Mitchell Field on Long Island he entertained wounded who had been flown in from London; at Hunter College in the Bronx he was swarmed over by 3,000 screaming, hysterical WAVES.

And one out of all those 3,000 lady sailors had the nerve to rush up to Coop, throw her arms around his neck, and kiss him.

"By golly," said Gary, blushing, "I didn't know the Navy was so much fun."

Then Coop took the WAVE in his arms and kissed her back.

The shrieks of 3,000 females in blue was deafening.

That was Coop during the war: a star tall in stature, tall in everyone's esteem, admired and revered by all.

CHAPTER SIXTEEN

Gary Cuts Up as a Producer

In a moment of perspicacity, when he was thinking back upon his life over those years of World War II, Gary Cooper admitted to himself that he had been pretty serious during that time, perhaps too serious in too many matters.

He did, of course, have moments of fun and laughter, but the vital, carefree abandon that any person of creativity must have from time to time, like a cool green oasis in the sun-bleached desert, simply hadn't been part of his experience during those long years he had labored so strenuously for Hollywood's film moguls. He hadn't been soured by the war. He knew that. But he'd been unable to grasp the new postwar perspective. What he needed, although he admitted he didn't recognize the need at the time, was another stretch of solitude. He'd done it several times in the past — walked away alone to come to terms with his soul — and it worked, notably in the early thirties when he went off to Africa.

There was a difference now, however. In the past he

recognized the need for a long walk. Now, he could only grope.

Life, and his work, had to go on the way it was, at least for the present.

Cooper had gotten into this mood after a rugged three years of wartime, during which he not only had contributed his services to entertaining troops in person, but had also engaged in a full, backbreaking schedule of picture making.

After *Pride of the Yankees*, Paramount became interested in a novel that Ernest Hemingway had written, which Gary Cooper sent to the studio for its consideration as a movie. The novel was titled *For Whom the Bell Tolls*. Sam Wood went for it in a big way, and, ignoring Cooper who had put him in touch with the script, promptly launched a major talent search that threatened to give David O. Selznick's celebrated quest for an actress to play Scarlett O'Hara some stiff competition. Practically every big-name player in Hollywood, and a few dozen lesser lights, was mentioned as a likely prospect for one of the choice roles in this picture. Some were even screen-tested. But when the final choices were made, it was Gary Cooper as Robert Jordan and Ingrid Bergman to play the short-haired, affectionate Maria. These two stars, by the way, had been author Hemingway's choices right from the start for the two most important roles in this story of the Spanish Civil War.

"The screen has met the challenge of fine literature triumphantly," wrote Howard Barnes, the New York *Herald Tribune* movie critic, after viewing the picture at the Rivoli. "Gary Cooper and Ingrid Bergman play starring roles with the true stature and authority of stars, while the supporting cast is never far behind them and sometimes a step ahead. .... There is no end of splendid acting in the film."

After *For Whom the Bell Tolls*, Gary Cooper abandoned the strong and silent film character he was best known for and took the part of a fumbling cowboy, unlike anything Coop had ever done — but more about that in a moment.

He went on to do *The Story of Dr. Wassell*, a wartime epic about Dr. Corydon M. Wassell, the naval medical officer whose exploits — in getting a group of wounded sailors safely out of Java while the Japanese were trying to stop them with machine-gun bullets — were first brought to the public's attention by President Franklin Delano Roosevelt in a radio report on the war shortly after Pearl Harbor.

The President's voice hardly had faded from the airwaves before Cecil B. DeMille decided to make Dr. Wassell's exploits the basis of a Paramount movie. Once again Coop proved that he could step into another man's shoes and depict his life accurately, dramatically, honestly.

Coop had always been honest in every endeavor he undertook, even in the small things in which many other Hollywood stars are prone to exercise less than complete integrity, such as in interviews with writers. Being in a business of pretending, many Hollywood stars allow press agents and studio flacks to issue statements to newspapers and magazines that the stars themselves never uttered.

Gary always insisted on speaking for himself in his own words — except perhaps this one time when he allowed someone to write his script. And the result was a sobering experience for him.

It happened during the 1944 Presidential campaign when Franklin Roosevelt was running for an unprecedented fourth term. His opponent was Thomas E. Dewey, the young Republican governor of New York. The Republican National Committee was rounding up the Hollywood film colony in its corner, zeroing in principally on big-name stars who formerly had backed Roosevelt. Coop was one prize the committee garnered. He was asked to go on radio and read a statement prepared by the committee's writers, a five-minute pro-Dewey speech. Coop agreed, and he spoke after the Bob Hope program was cut short by five minutes to make the paid political airtime available for this purpose.

After he spoke over the network, the GOP bought space in newspapers all over the country and reprinted the speech. The New York *Times* of November 6, 1944 — the day before the election — was one of the papers that carried the paid political advertisement, fifteen inches deep across three columns. There was a large picture of a serious-faced Gary Cooper and a 48-point headline reading, "I've been for Roosevelt before ... BUT NOT THIS TIME." The text went as follows:

"All of us have a great stake in this election and that's why all of us have been worrying — more than most times, I think — about how we should vote. For my own self, here's how I came to my own conclusion and here's what it is. I am going to vote for Governor Dewey because he's efficient — and, because he's honest. That's terribly important, I think, his being honest. Matter of fact, I've been for Mr. Roosevelt before — but not this time. There's been too many broken promises to suit me — and too much double talk.

"I was born in Helena, Montana, and every year along about this time — election time — I get to thinking about the people I grew up with, the men and women that had the same education I had — and that had the same principles drilled into them for judging public officials that I had. I have a feeling that they've all been trying their best —

like I have — to figure out how to cast their votes where they'll do the most good for this country that's done so much for all of us. And that means to me, the way I'm sure it does to them, that first of all the man we vote for has got to be honest. That's Governor Dewey, to my mind. And there's another thing I was wondering how to put it into words — until an old friend of mine put it into words for me the other day. He's fixing up an old saddle of mine and we got to talking about the election and I said to him:

"Cap, I guess you're going to vote for Roosevelt again this year. Huh?' And he looked at me and said 'Nope, not this time. I don't like the company he's keeping.'

"I disagree with the New Deal belief that the America all of us love is old and worn-out and finished — and has to borrow foreign notions that don't even seem to work any too well where they come from. I agree with Governor Dewey that our country is a young country that just has to make up its mind to be itself again. It can be itself again, if Governor Dewey is elected. And that's why I think it's time for a change."

The ad was paid for by the Republican National Committee in New York City.

The public's reaction was almost instantaneous. Readers poured letters of protest into their newspapers, calling Coop to task, not so much for standing opposed to Roosevelt but for the language he used — which few persons believed was his. The writers criticized Coop for two key phrases — "the company he (Roosevelt) keeps" and the bit about being opposed to "foreign" ideas.

Here are typical comments from letters-to-the-editor columns:

"The greatest shock I received was when I heard the word 'foreign' come from your mouth," wrote a reader from Manhattan in a letter addressed to Coop. "For some reason or other I always felt you were a real American. Mr. Cooper, just what constitutes a 'foreigner'? Can you explain? Personally, Mr. Cooper, my own parents came here from Romania more than 60 years ago. I consider myself a true and good American."

Another reader, from Newark, N. J., wrote:

". . .Came as quite a shock to me, after having seen Gary Cooper portray the common man and the true democrat in his pictures, *Mr. Deeds, Sergeant York*, and especially and most recently Robert Jordan in *For Whom the Bell Tolls*. . . . Evidently the people who write his movie scripts and those who write his political speeches come from different sides of the track."

Coop did not say anything about the criticism. Of course, millions cheered Gary for stating his political beliefs — but millions also had been aroused by Coop's choice of words, which the majority of critics, even pro-Dewey voters, could not believe were his own.

Though Coop had not become a Roosevelt hater, he was a Republican, had his convictions about Dewey, and had gone on the air to say why — even if not in his own words. The hundreds of abusive and critical letters that were written to him directly by indignant fans baffled Gary.

But he never regretted the position he took.

Some observers have said that the reason for the violent reaction to his radio talk against Roosevelt was that the public had been mesmerized by Coop's long silences and reputation as a quiet man. They had come to believe that Gary was incapable of having an opinion of his own.

The public soon forgot Coop's political convictions and recentered its attentions on his screen activities.

Coop galloped back to familiar territory — the good old West — in the film *Along Came Jones*. However, his portrayal of Melody Jones, a singing cowboy, was probably his most unconvincing role. Incredibly, despite his stature, this one film brought him nearer to the brink of failure than he had ever been before.

At this time of his life now, at the age of 45, Coop had become obsessed with the notion that the vital factor determining whether a film would be a hit or a flop was the actor himself and his knowledge of his part.

His self-assurance about the truthfulness of this belief lured him into forming a company named International Pictures, Inc. William Goetz was president and his partner, Leo Spitz, served as the board of directors, as Coop put it. Nunnally Johnson, the noted author and screenwriter, was picked as the writer–producer of the picture the company would make.

Operations began on Producers' Row of the Goldwyn Studios, where the infant company rented a sound stage and executive suites.

"Until Gary Cooper came along, nobody in Hollywood had ever thought of tall producers," said Nunnally Johnson in recalling his experience with Coop. "The very notion had the ring of a paradox, like a gloomy fat girl, or a comedian who smokes cigarettes."

The long and short of it, as Johnson emphasized, is that a producer has to come up with a story likely to interest at least half the people in the United States.

"He must also manage its conversation into a screen play which tells that story without wasting time about it. He must cast this screen play with actors and actresses or reasonable facsimiles. He must engage a director, a cameraman, and a small army of technical experts. And, too, no great harm is done if he can also show a little dough."

Coop's choice of story was *Along Came Jones*, adapted from a good-humored Western story by Alan LeMay.

"Every two or three years," said Johnson, "the smell of

the purple sage would get into Coop's nostrils and nothing would do but he had to break out his old boots and saddle and gallop down the shortcut to head 'em off at Eagle Pass."

So his choice of *Along Came Jones* was hardly unexpected.

But before a picture can be filmed, an executive has to have an office. Coop had ensconced himself in impressive surroundings. There was the usual mahogany desk with its specially engraved metal nameplate and battery of telephones.

Trophies and pictures attesting to Gary's association with filmdom's producing problems and their successful solutions adorned the walls.

A row of filing cabinets bulged with sheaves of papers — costume designs, lighting blueprints, cost sheets, expense accounts.

What couldn't be stuffed into these receptacles overflowed onto Gary's desk in a tangled mess that would soon grow uncontrollable.

His secretary flitted in and out, exchanging memos on a thousand and one items, sometimes bearing a glass of water and a couple of aspirins to relieve the boss's throbbing headaches.

No help for the mounting migraine was the continuous jangling of the telephone.

Johnson said that Coop breezed through the first few weeks as producer like an old hand.

"In the natural course of events," Nunnally related, "Coop flashed his greenbacks and signed up Loretta Young, a Western-type lady, among her other accomplishments."

Bill Demarest was also signed, along with Dan Duryea.

"So far," said Johnson, "it was a breeze. In fact, the only

problem at all during these preparations, the selection of a male star to play the part of Melody Jones and snuggle up to Loretta Young in the last ten feet of film, was quickly resolved through an unexpected and happy inspiration. The script called for a very tall, handsome, outdoor type, with a quiet, forceful personality and an ability to ride and make love convincingly. Elaborate plans for a nationwide search for such an actor had hardly been drawn up when somebody in the company (Mr. Cooper) pointed out that the producer himself came pretty near fitting that description — a neat and hugely satisfactory solution to what threatened at first to be a long, tedious, and expensive operation.

"It is ideas like this that mark the alert, on-his-toes type of producer."

It was only when production actually reached the stage of "shooting with gun and camera simultaneously," said Johnson, that Coop showed his mettle. The acid test was the day the designer brought Coop sketches for Loretta Young's wardrobe, a selection of garments that a simple ranch maid would wear. Gary looked at the drawings, was about to initial them, when he suddenly sensed his obligation to his new role as producer.

"How much?" inquired Coop.

"Average about $175 apiece," replied the designer.

Coop mulled over the drawings some more.

"Supposed to be cheap store dresses, aren't they?"

"Yes, sir."

"Kind that cost about $7.50?"

"Yes, sir."

"Then why don't we just go down to some cheap store and buy them for that?"

"We can," replied the designer, "but I'd appreciate it very much if you'd go yourself to Miss Young and be the one to inform her of this new arrangement."

Johnson reported that for a moment there was dead silence.

"This was it, the first clearcut test of the man as producer, and every eye was on him," Nunnally said. "Then came the decision, not hastily but weighed and balanced and with the firm, sure touch of the born executive."

" 'Oh never mind,' " Johnson reported Coop as mumbling, " 'these'll be all right.' " And he initialed the drawings.

"It was a small thing, no doubt," Nunnally quipped, "but it showed the fundamental strength of the man, and there were smiles of pride on the faces of his associates, for they knew the kind of leader they had. And their heads were high and their eyes bright."

As the picture was being made, Gary found himself on a mill wheel of production difficulties. Every step of progress was cancelled out by yet another snafu.

There came a day when Gary's ears ached from listening to the problems of the director, the art director, casting director, makeup man, film editor, head nurse, prop man, chief electrician, dressing room custodian, the unit man, and a dozen others.

"I soon learned that delays are not only dangerous, they're downright expensive," Coop once opined.

He sweated out several hundred dollars worth of peace of mind on one occasion when a lighting failure held up filming while technicians traced the trouble to a tiny break in a circuit.

"Everybody was calm, cool, and collected during the catastrophe, except me," Gary said. "After all, why shouldn't they be? The pay was still rolling in, even though we were all in the dark. The loss was all my pleasure,"

Gary began to develop a gaping split in personality, torn

between his duties as leading man and his obligation as an executive and producer. "Don't let the job get you down," Johnson said in his rich, drawlin' Georgia accent. "Life's too short fr'all that."

It was just about the most unconvincing advice Cooper had gotten in his life, which he was becoming increasingly convinced was much too long — at least some days were.

"I began to sense that I wasn't the most suitably adapted to the job," he said. "It seemed to require the money of a Midas, the brain of an Aristotle, the strength of a Hercules, and the fortitude of Job. And that was a tall order.

"I don't think I entirely filled the bill. I found myself counting dollar signs instead of sheep to get to sleep. It was quite a terrifying experience. All those dollar signs."

Eventually it dawned on Coop that, in the hectic, flamboyant ways of Hollywood, the logical, levelheaded approach was not necessarily the right one, and that the best outlook was constantly to expect the unexpected.

For instance, how could Coop for the life of him know that Dan Costello, a veteran of a dozen Westerns, couldn't even get himself into the saddle of a horse?

Gary could have ended all his torments by arranging with the prop man to have some live cartridges slipped into the six-shooter of a gun-duel opponent while his own hardware remained loaded with blanks. But no. Coop decided that might be a little too flamboyant.

Gary Cooper finally learned that a motion picture doesn't begin and end with the actor, no matter how towering his self-assurance.

He had a strong suspicion that with all the work, all the confusion, the thousand items that go into producing a picture, the actor was really a nuisance. Lucky to be allowed on the set.

His problems mounted. There was, for example, the knotty little thing about his salary as an actor versus his responsibilities as a producer with a budget to adhere to. As a producer, and a raw bushleaguer at that, Coop was finding that he had to devote most of his time to the production end of his films. That was bad enough for a man of Coop's temperament, but when he reflected that he was paying himself as an actor, and losing thousands of dollars because he couldn't devote as much time as an actor should, it was enough to drive him to distraction. In one particularly dark mood, he was heard to mumble:

"If I can't earn my pay acting, I'm gonna fire me."

And so it went, and when Johnson says it was untrue that there was any more chaos on his set while making *Along Came Jones* than there generally is on any other, then Nunnally's word must be taken as gospel.

Nevertheless, the hectic pace of producing raised doubts in Gary about his future as an executive. It wasn't simply a matter of not feeling temperamentally suited to producing that made him skeptical, but the uncomfortable feeling that he had somehow allowed his judgment to go awry. In trying to succeed as a producer, he had failed himself as an actor.

In *Along Came Jones*, Coop was the antithesis of his usual strong hero. He was, actually, a grotesque caricature of all the roles he had played in the past, a stumbling, inept, foolish cowboy who not only drops his guns whenever he draws, but who, in the absurd end, has to be saved by the heroine rather than vice versa.

A short while after *Along Came Jones* was released, Coop met Cecil B. DeMille at a party.

"That's not you up there on the screen, Gary," DeMille cautioned Coop. "Not you at all. You've let yourself down, but more importantly you've let your public down. And that's dangerous. You can do it once, and they'll forgive you. But don't do it a second time."

Coop appreciated DeMille's concern. But he plunged

right into a second bad film, *Casanova Brown*, which he also produced under the banner of International Pictures. This time he was the buffoon, involved in a slapstick situation more suitable for a Three Stooges movie.

One amusing anecdote during production on this film was related by Charles Samuels, the Hollywood writer. Someone, it seems, had told Coop that he ought to throw more weight around — especially with Johnson. Gary was told to prod Nunnally, or he'd start to lie down on the job.

"Get Nunnally on the phone," Samuels reported Coop was told. "Ask him what he's done, tell him he should have written more by this time. Give it to him with both barrels."

Cooper rushed to the phone and called Johnson while the others listened.

"Hello, Nunnally," said Gary, "this is Coop. How are you? How's your wife? How's that story getting along?"

"Fine," said Johnson.

"Gee, that's great," Coop replied. "Keep up the good work, Nunnally."

Then, Samuels said, Coop came back to the others and announced:

"It's fun to bawl writers out."

It's quite evident Coop wasn't cut out to be a movie producer, a fact he often admitted himself in later years. So it came to pass that he quit that side of the business after letting down his public — not once as DeMille had admonished, but twice. But since he had delivered so many first-rate films in the past, and because he was the beloved and great Gary Cooper, they forgot about it.

But Gary himself didn't. He threw himself into a succession of new and exciting roles in *Cloak and Dagger, Unconquered, Good Sam, The Fountainhead, Task Force, Bright Leaf, Dallas, You're in the Navy Now,* and *Saratoga*

Trunk, which reunited him, happily, with Ingrid Bergman.

All of them were good. Some were memorable.

Saratoga Trunk was probably the best of the lot. Although Gary and Ingrid could not reach the exhilarating and dramatic heights of *For Whom the Bell Tolls*, they nevertheless gave first-rate performances as Colonel Clint Maroon, a long, lanky con man from Texas, and Clio Dulaine, a beautiful Creole girl. The setting, in President Grant's post-Civil War era, was highlighted by a railroad feud with work gangs fighting among themselves.

Their appearance in a film together again also gave rise to rumors of a "romance" between Gary and Ingrid, but the evidence does not support such a belief too strongly. They were friendly, of course. They were seen together a lot on the set, but that was to be expected of two stars sharing the leads and the chief love interest in the film.

In *Unconquered*, Coop again worked with Cecil B. De-Mille, the great master of the epic movie.

A $4,000,000 extravaganza, *Unconquered* premiered in October, 1947, but received universally so-so reviews. Some of the critics, perhaps stunned by the immense, overwhelming action of the film, simply synopsized the plot for their readers and let it go at that. The *Times'* usually pithy reviewer, Bosley Crowther, deciding he had to say *something* that hinted of a critical judgment, finally concluded that *Unconquered* was worth seeing "if for nothing else but laughs."

Coop, riding high on a new wave of popularity and financial security, continued to pick and choose his films. He selected two pictures to do in 1948 — a bright comedy called *Good Sam*, and a long, ponderous, philosophic drama called *The Fountainhead*.

In *Good Sam* he worked with the ebullient Ann Sheridan and Gary felt this film once more fulfilled the dimensions of the Gary Cooper his public had come to respect and admire.

The Fountainhead was a story of dramatic might and brooding power, the screen adaptation of Ayn Rand's runaway best-seller of the same name.

Gary Cooper didn't know it at the time, but *The Fountainhead* was to become a crucial, dramatic turning point in his private life.

CHAPTER SEVENTEEN

The Man Who Must Take a Long Walk

It began innocently enough. Gary Cooper had read and liked the script Ayn Rand had adapted from her own novel, *The Fountainhead*.

Ironically, it was Rocky who first brought Cooper's attention to the story.

"My wife read the book when it came out," Gary told an interviewer. "She suggested that I might want to do it as a picture. I thought it quite a controversial story and I could visualize a lot of people resenting it. That was good. If they were interested, pro or con, it meant they would get excited by it and tell other people to see it.

"It had a good love interest. If my leading lady, Patricia Neal's character in the picture was inconsistent, it was no more inconsistent than most women are in real life."

Coop agreed to portray Howard Roark, an unbending, scrupulously honest and incorruptible architect dedicated to the rights of the individual. It was a solid, meaty part and Coop was eminently satisfied that his leading lady was to be Patricia Neal, a tall, willowy blonde who had made a name for herself on the Broadway stage.

"I took the part because I had a lot of curiosity about it," said Coop. "This story says, 'Maybe you're doing a fellow a lot of harm in giving him everything. Maybe he ought to stand on his own feet and reach out for what he wants . . . he can't harm anyone if he fights for what he thinks is his duty in life.' "

In time the words Coop spoke would take on great significance. Coop seemed to follow through on this theme and thinking.

He hit it off immediately with Patricia. Coop, the essentially shy, introverted man, Pat Neal, the sensitive, intelligent young woman. They worked hard and diligently at *The Fountainhead*, a film rather difficult to create because of its structural lack of action. It was a movie of ideas rather than of action and it demanded an extra measure of emotion from all its performers.

The finished picture turned out to be a rather cheerless thing. It was mercilessly clobbered by nearly every critic. But it was evident to everyone that Coop and Pat had reached an extraordinary rapport with one another professionally, and they promptly went into a second film called *Bright Leaf.* The year was now 1949.

The rapport, once limited to their professional lives, expanded almost inevitably to their personal lives. They found common interests, lost themselves in deep, absorbing conversation, dined together, and began acting, as one executive on the picture put it, "like a couple of fourteen-year-olds on a park bench."

Everyone who knew Coop intimately agreed that he was totally entranced by the striking blonde. Was it love? As the word is used in Hollywood, yes, everyone said, it was love. Was it a permanent kind of love? Was it marriage love? There the confusion set in.

Nobody knew. And least of all Coop himself.

In order to marry Pat Neal, Gary would have to divorce Rocky. That would dislocate seventeen years of marriage — a marriage that, like everyone else's, had had its good moments and its bad — its fights, its furies, its love and laughter, and, occasionally, its moments of absolute boredom and disenchantment.

Unlike most marriages, though, the Cooper marriage was endowed with an extraordinary *laissez faire* attitude on both sides that allowed Coop and Rocky to roam alone pretty much as they wished and to insulate each of them within mutually exclusive worlds that the other could not or would not enter. That loose arrangement freed — if that's the word — Gary to carry on his relationship with Pat.

Indeed, so oddly unreal was the Cooper marriage in that respect that the movie columnists were calling it "the most amazing marriage in Hollywood."

The anecdotes, some apocryphal, some very genuine, that emerged from the marriage, are legion.

One close friend of the family, in talking of the incident later, said that the image of Veronica Cooper staying home and weeping while Gary was seeing Patricia Neal was downright "laughable."

"Rocky? Pining away? God, how absurd," he said — and here was a man who had known both for fifteen years. "Try to remember, if you can, all the parties Rocky went to while Coop was cavorting down in Cuba with Pat that time they went to see Hemingway. I bet you can't recall. Dozens, I'd say. And she'd be dancing with different men at every single one of them. That's to say nothing of the ski trips she made, and the rides out in the country with this guy or that. Don't worry about Rocky. Her pining for Coop? That's laughable."

He wasn't saying that Rocky was no longer in love with Coop, or that he cared nothing for her. It's simply that when either had a gap to fill — a gap created by the temporary absence of the other — each filled it by letting more of the outside world into his or her private world.

The truth was that Rocky and Coop actually did see a great deal of each other. They weren't constantly in flight from one another.

Joan Crawford, describing some of the Cooper "togetherness," tells of the "great camaraderie" that frequently existed between the two.

"When Gary was not in a picture," Miss Crawford said, "He arranged his business appointments so that they'd have all their meals together and spend their free time by themselves. During the year they'd give two or three large parties which they'd planned together."

Rocky usually cooked Gary's breakfast — a whopping affair always — and in the evenings they'd usually dine out at least twice a week.

Conversations frequently dealt with Coop's work, Miss Crawford revealed. She quoted Gary as saying, "I value Rocky's reaction on stories very highly because she has such a detached point of view. She's not confused by the mechanics of a script and can get a clear idea of drama in a story without being sidetracked by camera or stage directions."

Yet even Miss Crawford saw into Coop's nature enough to perceive there the unslakable thirst for solitude.

"When Gary got a day off from work," she said, "he enjoyed going out for long walks by himself. While most men liked to go out with the boys, Gary preferred being alone. He enjoyed hunting, fishing, riding, and walking without company. He did not seem to need the stimulus of people to enjoy himself. Nor did he like being conspicuous. He had good taste in clothes and had all that any man required, but he still preferred the informality of blue jeans and leather jackets. He had a theory that if you go on about your business like Joe Doakes, you won't be recognized; and if you are, the recognition will come too late for people to stop and mob you."

All very true. There was indeed a great camaraderie between Gary and Rocky, but it was those temporary absences that merited their marriage its "most amazing" sobriquet.

There was, for example, the time Coop was in Europe working on a picture. Almost daily the press boldly chronicled his date with this English beauty or that French actress, and never once did Coop object, or, more important, stop dating the girls.

And Rocky? Well, back in Hollywood, Rocky was seeing Rock Hudson, Peter Lawford, and, on one occasion, even young Robert Wagner. Again, all of it was recorded in the Hollywood gossip columns.

"I don't know what to make of those two," a studio executive once said after watching a remarkable demonstration of their unique live-and-let-live attitude at a dinner party.

"What goes with the man? Here we're all sitting around after dinner and Gary glances at his watch and nonchalantly strolls out the door with a polite good night. And Veronica watches him go, knowing full well his heart belongs outside the home and seemingly she couldn't care less."

The studio executive had been a witness to the way the Coopers put their unusual code into action. There were other observers, even more puzzled.

Writer Jean Ward, for instance, tells of the report that had Gary and Rocky at the same famous ski resort at the same time — but not together. . . .

They had arrived separately, occupied separate rooms and moved around in their own whirlwind group of men and women. And then, to confuse matters, they'd spot one another, kiss each other publicly, perhaps ski together for an hour, and drift off, each to his own little group. As Miss Ward tells it, "one story had it that an Old Westbury, Long Island, social lion dogged Rocky's ski tracks and begged her to get a divorce and marry him. A stunning pair of diamond earrings supposedly commemorates the proposal."

Society columnist Igor Cassini, in his "Cholly Knicker-bocker" column in the New York *Journal-American*, went further at the time by identifying Howell van Gerbig, former All-American athlete, as the Old Westburyite who was courting Mrs. Cooper.

Cassini called it "the hottest romance this hot summer (1951)."

The columnist said that "during the whole summer Mrs. Cooper and van Gerbig were inseparable in Southampton, L. I. . . . As a matter of fact, many of Rocky's and Van's friends are already talking about the possibility of marriage, despite the fact that the appealing Mrs. Cooper is supposed to have stated a few months ago that she would never give Gary a divorce."

And so the episodes went — or at least the retelling of them. Gary with his own clique . . . Rocky with hers. Gary going out with a bevy of young beauties; Rocky seeing this distinguished financier, that handsomely suave actor. And all the while carrying it out with a certain dignity and respectability that kept their marriage intact and armored them both from accusations of tawdriness. The marriage might have been "amazing" but not a mockery and certainly not sordid.

A friend of the Coopers — perhaps among the two or three persons closest to both — summed up the marriage this way:

"I sincerely believe marriage between Gary and Rocky became a thing of competition, rather than a sharing. It may not have been a conscious arrangement, but nevertheless I think it existed.

"You see, Rocky is a woman who wants to be best in everything. She threw herself wholeheartedly into every sport Gary loved, not with the feeling of companionship so much as besting and winning. She became an expert in skeet-shooting, at swimming, and in time surpassed Gary at skiing. An ailing back and the complications of his broken hip from his younger days slowed Gary and gave Rocky the lead.

"She began plunging into the icy Pacific every morning to preserve the firmness of her body and eventually induced Gary to take these swims with her. In time it was Rocky who was leading and Gary following.

"I really believe it was Rocky's determination to be best and have the best that prompted her to 'collect' Gary. Even then he was the best, the most eligible of men."

Another friend supports that theory.

"I know Rocky came from New York's Park Avenue–Southampton set," he said, "but even so, Coop must have looked mighty attractive to her. A good catch. Look at it this way. Coop was tall and handsome with that boyish appeal that women go for whether they're from Southampton or South Brooklyn.

"And then, too, he had a reputation as a lover. That must surely have made Rocky interested in him. They were still spinning some of those torrid yarns about Coop and Lupe Velez about the time Rocky met him and you can bet she heard about them. But there were a lot of others, too. Clara Bow and most especially the Countess di Frasso, whom Rocky ultimately met and gave her walking papers.

"Take everything together — Coop's good looks, charm, his reputation, his zooming acting career — and any woman would be happy to 'collect' him."

Nevertheless, Veronica Balfe could not have married Gary Cooper unless Gary himself was willing. Love would have made him want Rocky as his bride, certainly, but a good friend of Coop's has another idea.

"He was ready for it. Period," said the friend. "He was tired of tomcatting around. He'd had his fill of casual romances and was ready for security, home, marriage, kids, the whole bit. My point is that he was at that point conditioned to tumble. Rocky entered his life at the precise moment he was ripe for it. He hit it off better with Rocky than with the other girls he was going with. And bam! They got married. But it could just as easily have been someone else."

At any rate, they wed, and the marriage — that "amazing" marriage — stayed together. And it stayed together for a variety of reasons. Rocky was a Catholic and opposed to divorce. They had Maria, a darkly beautiful girl about whom Gary once said, "She is my life." They had a genuine feeling for one another, a comfortable feeling. And finally, there apparently had been no new love in either of their lives to warrant a divorce.

Until Coop made *The Fountainhead* and met Patricia Neal.

Now, for the first time in seventeen years, Gary Cooper was confused emotionally. Was his feeling for Pat Neal irrational, momentary, an insignificant fixation? He wasn't sure. Was he simply restless? Was he anxious now for freedom just as he had been anxious for marriage seventeen years earlier? Did he need a new freedom from Rocky and the home they had built across nearly two decades? He wasn't sure.

It was time, he told himself, for another long walk, and deep, deep reflection. His marriage to Rocky had given him a sense of security. Did he want to demolish it?

Coop did take his long walk, figuratively, and dwelled at length on the emotional turmoil within him.

And then in 1950, while *Bright Leaf,* his second film with Pat Neal, was still on view in the movie houses around the country, Coop went to Rocky and asked for a separation.

The facts actually came out much later. At the time, November, 1950, Coop told newsmen, who had been tipped off that something in the big Brentwood home was wrong, that it was all nothing more than "a little difficulty."

"I can't say we haven't had a little difficulty, but I can say that it isn't serious," Coop declared. "I hope to finish the picture I'm on, then I'm going to New York to spend Christmas with Rocky and Maria and talk things over."

Veronica herself a day later confirmed the separation but emphasized:

"I'm a Catholic and under no circumstances would I ever make any plans for a divorce. I came to New York to give Gary a chance to think things over."

Six months later, Gary had evidently thought things out fully and had come to his conclusion. On the evening of May 6, 1951, Graham Sterling, Rocky's attorney, announced crisply in Hollywood that Gary and his wife had agreed on a separation and that negotiations for a property settlement were under way.

Now it was official. The long marriage between the Montana cowboy and the Park Avenue socialite was at the brink of the abyss.

Coop maintained a typical silence, but the breakup and the reasons for it were candidly told by Pat Neal in a revealing interview with Hollywood columnist Hedda Hopper, Coop's long time friend. The occasion, curiously enough, was also the breakup of Pat's and Gary's romantic interlude.

"I will not see him when I go back to Hollywood," Pat told Hedda in New York. "I have been very much in love with him. And I am sure he has loved me. But I saw that it wouldn't work so I stepped out. I have a lot of life ahead of me. And I want to live it with someone who is fun and unentangled, someone with whom I can have a relationship that will be good — and permanent.

"Coop is wonderful. I never knew anybody like him. But he's a very complex person, as you well know. We last saw each other on Christmas Eve — briefly. It is, I assure you, over and ended forever. Wouldn't you know it would be just my luck to fall in love with a married man?"

It was only after Pat Neal walked out of Coop's life that the details of their romance began to be filled in.

Pat had fallen in love with Coop, according to Hedda, during the production of *The Fountainhead* back in 1949.

"It was not, however, until 1950, after he and Miss Neal did *Bright Leaf,* that Gary asked Rocky for a separation," Hedda wrote.

"Never, Rocky insists, had Coop asked for a divorce. After this, Coop and Pat were glimpsed occasionally at restaurants. But not until much later, when their romance had come into the open, did they ever attend parties together."

It was at one of the parties that Hedda saw the first sign

that Coop and Pat were heading for a breakup. The party was thrown by Charles Feldman for Dolly O'Brien, one of Clark Gable's earlier girlfriends.

"It was one of their [Coop's and Pat's] first party appearances," Hedda said. "When they came in they went directly to the end of the bar. There they remained until dinner was announced. Rocky, on the other hand, arrived with Peter Lawford, and went immediately to the table assigned her. I was sorry Pat didn't look pretty that night. She wore flowers in her hair, like an ingenue. They didn't become her. Rocky, in contrast, being a sophisticated woman of the world, and having all the cards in her hand, was very gay, danced every dance, and never took the smile off her face.

"At about midnight, when Pat was dancing, Coop got up and, for a few minutes, visited Rocky's table. Everyone held his breath. I would not be surprised if it was then and there that Pat accepted the fact that things would not work out and so — stepped out."

Whether or not that was the precise "moment of truth" for Pat Neal, by Christmas Eve 1951, she was determined not to see Coop again and she left for Georgia to visit her parents and to put a whole continent between Gary Cooper and her aching heart.

And Coop?

The tall, confused actor was left, according to intimates, with a "terrible torch" for Pat.

But in her own desolation she had fled, and Rocky was gone now, and Coop, bereft of his past home ties and uncertain of the future, embarked on what for him, perhaps, were the longest, loneliest years of his life.

The Uncertain Years

Once before, two long, history-filled decades earlier, Gary Cooper had taken flight from the fearful tensions of Hollywood by crossing the gangplank of an ocean liner and sailing for Europe.

Now, in his painful period of inner conflict, Coop was again in flight, and again his destination was Europe.

He departed for the Continent in the summer of 1951, but not before he had completed work on a film that was destined to catapult him to the greatest pinnacle of his professional career.

Throughout all his terrible time of indecision and divided emotion, Coop had continued to appear in a string of movies.

But with the exception of *Task Force* — a mighty semi-documentary epic that traced the agonizing expansion of the Navy's air arm — in which he costarred with Jane Wyatt, none of the films was satisfactory to him. His public had begun to feel ever so slightly let down, but they still loved him, they still admired him, they still went to see his pictures, good, bad or indifferent.

There had been *Dallas*, a 1950 piece of mediocrity in which, with Ruth Roman decorating the screen every other scene or so, he portrayed an ex-Confederate colonel on the lam. Through a clichéd plot twist, Coop posed as a U. S. marshal and cleaned up Dallas by sweeping it clean of the Marlow Brothers, a vicious trio whose first names were — if one is gullible enough to believe it — William, Cullen, and Bryant.

There was *Distant Drums*, issued in 1951. Shaking loose the Dallas dust, Coop donned a pair of buckskins and headed for the Florida Everglades as a backwoodsman, to knock off a gang of smugglers.

And then there followed swiftly, all issued in that waste-of-time year of 1951, *It's a Big Country, Starlift*, and *You're in the Navy Now*.

None of them gave Coop the feeling of achievement he had known in the days of his better works. His private life had been sundered by an emotional schism, and now his professional life seemed to be following a parallel course of disintegration. Coop was too thoroughly the seasoned pro to panic, but he did begin to read very carefully the avalanche of scripts that came his way. The standard, trite old formula Westerns were out. So were any other stories that failed to portray him in the image he knew his public liked and demanded. He did not know specifically what sort of script he wanted as his next venture. He knew only that when he saw it, he would recognize it.

And it finally came from Stanley Kramer. Its title: *High Noon*. Coop knew instinctively it was tailor-made for him and he for it.

To a friend in New York, Coop said:

"When I received the script, I took one read of it and

knew it was a natural for me. My dad used to sit me on his knee and tell me stories about the sheriffs he dealt with in his days on the Montana Supreme Court bench, and all those episodes of the bygone years suddenly came back to me in full blossom right out of *High Noon.*

"My concept of a sheriff was that of a man who represented the people. Alone he could never do his job — he had to have help. The sheriff I was asked to play was different than any I'd ever known or heard about because Sheriff Kane had to stand alone, literally, against the lawless. It was a challenging role — and I loved it."

At another time, in an interview with William Pepe in the New York *World-Telegram & Sun,* Coop also added:

"Anyone who can read even a few words, me for instance, could have seen that was a good script."

High Noon, the story of Sheriff Will Kane, was the memorable tale of a town's cowardice and moral collapse. As Sheriff Kane, Coop finds himself the target of a vengeful gang that has vowed to kill him. In the beginning, the townspeople, with a hollow bravado, promise him all the help he needs. But as the moment of actual confrontation approaches and the prospect of gunfighting and a possible death becomes more menacing with every advancing minute, the people desert him one by one until, in the end, the sheriff faces his ordeal alone. Through canny thinking and quick shooting, he destroys three of the four outlaws who have come to kill him. Grace Kelly, his brand new bride in the film, kills the fourth one, although she is a Quaker and doesn't believe in killing.

And, now, with the would-be killers lying dead, in what surely must be one of the movie industry's greatest scenes, Coop looks about him as the townspeople rush out to congratulate him. Fixing each with a cold stare, he unpins his badge and drops it to the dirt. It is a gesture of naked, absolute contempt. Silently he escorts the young and exquisitely beautiful Miss Kelly into the wagon, and together they ride off.

High Noon was one of the greatest Westerns of all time and for it Gary Cooper won the 1952 Academy Award. His second!

"In *High Noon*," Coop said, "it was a part, like in Sergeant York, that took everything I had — and I gave it everything I had."

And the public gratefully accepted it. The not-always-easy-to-please *Times* critic, Bosley Crowther, became absolutely rhapsodic in his assessment of the picture.

"Every five years or so," he wrote, "somebody — somebody of talent and taste, with a full appreciation of legend and a strong trace of poetry in their soul — scoops up a handful of clichés from the vast lore of Western films and turns them into a thrilling and inspiring work of art in this genre. Such a rare and exciting achievement is Stanley Kramer's production of *High Noon*, which was placed on exhibition at the Mayfair Theater. . . . Mr. Cooper is at the top of his form in a type of role that has trickled like water off his back for years. . . . *High Noon* is a Western to challenge *Stagecoach* for the all-time championship."

Even before he had been awarded his second "Oscar," Coop's uneasy, restless spirit told him it was time for another of the long walks. In 1931, the African safari and the subsequent swing through Europe had mended his fractured spirit and restored his equanimity, and now once again Europe was issuing its voiceless summons.

He told Rocky of his plans, and on that summer day of 1951, the leathery actor, now 50, embarked on his journey.

He had no destination in mind. But Europe had served as an escape before. Why not again, he thought?

"It didn't work this time," Coop later recounted. "My

habit of taking a long walk which I had acquired back there on my family's ranch didn't seem to solve my problems this time. I found Gary Cooper could not just float off on a gondola in Venice as he did a couple of decades previously and be ignored.

"Now, as a celebrity, I was 'hot copy' to the newspapers. Everywhere I went I ran into reporters and photographers. They pursued me relentlessly. They hounded me for bulletins on my separation from Rocky — would we reconcile or divorce? If I happened to talk to a pretty actress or a model, the incident immediately was blown up into a romance."

The inability to flee, to conceal himself from a curious, prying, inquiring world grated at Coop's already frayed nerves.

"Being a movie star," he said, "has certain responsibilities. I owed a great deal to the public and was obliged to grant interviews and talk at times I didn't feel like saying anything. Sometimes I had to talk in a vacuum because I felt so listless and unenthused by the subjects brought up by the newshawks. I was trying to get away from it all and all I did was stew."

Stewing right along with him, apparently, in a furious boil, were his digestive juices. Coop, a notorious eater, now found himself unable even to nibble a bland soda cracker. In February, 1952, he went to a doctor in Europe and learned the mournful news.

"You are overworked," the doctor told him. "You have got what all high-tensioned actors get. You have an ulcer."

Whether it was from the high tension of his craft or from the inner tornadoes of indecision and worry about his family, Coop indeed did have a duodenal ulcer, and it so curtailed his activities that he had to return to the United States for treatment. He visited a doctor in New Orleans first, and he underwent further treatment at Roosevelt Hospital in New York City.

Then it was back to Hollywood to shoot a picture called *Springfield Rifle* and, shortly after that, in late 1952, to Samoa for some location shots for his role in James Michener's poignant *Return to Paradise.*

The ulcer was still with him, despite the small pharmacy of pills he was toting around.

When shooting on *Return to Paradise* was over, Coop drifted back to Hollywood and kicked around as a carefree bachelor. With Clark Gable or Bill Demarest or some of his other friends, he'd head for the high pheasant country of Idaho or the trout streams of the Sierra Nevadas. Back down on the lowlands of Hollywood and Vine, the peripatetic Gary Cooper occasionally would wander into a nightclub to party with this actress or that, and be "itemed" by the local gossip columnists, but none of the reported romances was real or even interesting to Coop.

Except for Patricia Neal, in fact, Coop remained singularly free of entanglement until the spring of 1953 when, back in Europe, he met and began to date a luscious French girl named Giselle Pascal.

An interesting tale hangs thereby, and it involves no less a personage than the suave and handsome Prince of Monaco, Ranier, who, it seemed, was outfoxed by a big, skinny cactus burr named Cooper.

As it was reported from Paris in that warm spring month of May, Cooper, still restless, still roaming, turned up at Cannes for the annual film festival.

In nearby Monaco, Giselle, a long-limbed beauty bronzed from the Mediterranean sun, was a guest of Ranier, and with his blessing, she tripped over to Cannes to see some of her old movie pals, since she used to be in the racket herself.

She gave Ranier a kiss on the cheek, the reports go, and told him, "I'll be home tonight, dear."

Alas, for Ranier, though, it was not to be. At a lunch that day, given by mutual friends, Coop and Giselle met and the sparks began to fly. Before anyone knew what had happened, Giselle was moving her place card to the table next to Coop.

The upshot, if anyone actually needs to be told, was that Giselle was a little late getting back to the palace. A week late, as a matter of fact.

And while Ranier was sitting up night after night, counting his chips in Monte Carlo, the two friends were having a traditional Riviera romance, eating snails and sipping champagne.

The film festival finally ended and Coop headed back to Paris, while Giselle went back to Monaco to pick up her things. She joined Gary in Paris where their romance was now becoming a little more noticeable.

Inevitably, the Paris reporters bloodhounded him down and asked Coop:

"What geeves weeth Giselle, M'sieu' Coopair? Weel you marry hair, yuh reckon?" — or words to that effect. Whereupon Coop responded:

"Miss Pascal is a nice girl, good company and a good dancer, too. But I don't know what all this hubbub is about.

"I was out with her only once since I have been in Paris. Tonight (May 21) was the second time. I go out with others, too. Miss Pascal is not the only one. I am not the favored one."

The first Paris date was an appearance at "The Ball of the Little White Beds" a few nights previously. One table companion said they held hands most of the evening and added that Coop appeared to be madly in love.

But the romance, if it had ever really reached that stage,

ended approximately then and there. On June 15,1953, Rocky and Maria visited Paris and Coop met his wife in what appeared to be a prelude to reconciliation.

It didn't happen then, but Gary and Rocky seemed to be moving closer and closer together. In November, 1953, for example, Coop returned to their home — as a guest.

There were other reported romances for the big actor, even while he and Rocky were trying to work out a reconciliation on a tentative basis.

One of them blazed across the headlines while Gary was in Mexico City making *Garden of Evil* with Richard Widmark. This time the papers had him linked to a beautiful San Antonio model named Lorraine Chanel.

Again came the Cooper disclaimer.

"Miss Chanel and I are friends, very good friends," Gary said. "But that's all there is to it. It doesn't seem to make any difference what I say, the gossip columnists seem to print whatever they want. But those who say I am going to marry Miss Chanel are wrong. All I'll say is that yes, I took Lorraine out . . . among others."

For all the Miss Chanels and "the others," Coop was steadily following the pathway to a reestablished home with Rocky and Maria.

One of the first hints came from a friend of Coop's, another famed actor. He was at a gala party that Gary and Rocky together tossed in their home — despite the fact they were estranged — and to which each had invited his own guests.

"You just have to look at Coop's face," the actor said, "and then you can stop wondering. He wants back."

Evidently the actor was right. The reconciliation came in the summer of 1954, when Coop, his wife and his daughter, unobtrusively and without press fanfare, went off to Southampton, where they now had a summer place of their own. A short while later they returned to Hollywood together and soon purchased an elegant home in the posh Holmby Hills area.

The nearly four-year-long "walk" that Gary Cooper had taken was at an end. He'd traveled along through Hollywood, New York, Cannes, Paris, London, Rome, Mexico, and even Samoa. He'd been tossed and buffeted by the capricious winds of life. His fortunes and his popularity soared — he'd been named the box-office king of 1953, he'd been awarded his second "Oscar." But with the ulcer his health had declined.

Because of the ubiquitous gossipers, he'd lost a little of the luster that had always attended his image. But he'd gained a new insight, a great new perspective. He'd come, finally, to an understanding with Rocky and, infinitely more important, himself.

Speaking with Louella Parsons, Coop said:

"You can't live with a woman seventeen years as I did with Rocky and not know all the good things about her. I have a lot of faults myself. Oh, sure, we both did things we perhaps shouldn't have done, and after that many years together there are moments when everyone feels he'd like a change."

Gary Cooper had come home.

The Final Years

"I learned a lot," Gary Cooper was saying, comfortably clad in an open-necked sports shirt and gray linen slacks, as he leaned back on the sofa in the beautifully furnished living room of his Holmby Hills house.

"Maybe I'm not over my bullheadedness. Perhaps I still have that stubbornness that led me to take off by myself on my walk to think things out. But I've come to realize one thing — you just can't keep running away. Sooner or later you've got to come back and face facts."

It was a late autumn day in 1956 and Coop was lounging about with an after-dinner drink in his hand.

Maria was in her bedroom, napping. Rocky was off visiting friends and would be back soon.

To an observer, Coop was that contented, peaceful man again, secure, 55 years old then, and perhaps showing it in the still-handsome face, but a fierce will to work and succeed was still with him. In a short while, *Friendly Persua-*

sion would be showing in movie houses the land over and Coop had only recently completed *The Court Martial of Billy Mitchell*, and before that *Vera Cruz*, and before that *Blowing Wild* and *Garden of Evil*.

The work had been constant and hard, but Coop had a look of tranquility.

"Hard work never killed anyone if that person had the good sense to combine some relaxation with it. I learned that way back in my early days in Hollywood; that's why I could put out like I did. Hunting, fishing, or just traveling are wonderful diversions and I've done them all. That's why I feel that I've led a full life. If I died tomorrow, I'd have no regrets — I've gotten satisfaction out of my life."

Rocky had come in the house by now and after giving Gary a quick, wifelike peck on the cheek, settled down next to him.

"And I don't mind the trips at all," she told the visitor. "I'm going to be adult about marriage. If Gary wants to go away, he's free to go wherever he wants. I'm never going to object. I think we both learned a lesson. It was worth waiting to have him come back."

They looked at one another and, as though both were possessed by the same thought at once, they extended their hands simultaneously and each gave the other a small, intimate squeeze.

One tiny gesture in one random afternoon of their lives, but it summed up the new love and life Gary and Rocky had found together.

And adding to the richness of their lives, of course, was their beautiful daughter, Maria.

Coop had remained eternally grateful to Rocky for rearing Maria so well during their years of separation. Soon after the reconciliation, Coop confided:

"Rocky has done a wonderful, wonderful job with

Maria. She has brought her up to be a deeply religious girl
— the finest young lady I know. . . ."

Not too many years later, when Maria was 23 and had
graduated from Marymount College, in the East, and went
on to art classes at the Chouinard Art Institute in Los
Angeles, she still was her dad's favorite girl and "pal."

Coop always regarded Maria as a levelheaded youngster
and in the latter years was more convinced than ever that
she was, because, as he put it:

"Now and then when I'd ask her to play a bit part in my
pictures, she'd refuse. . . ."

Rocky also seemed to have learned all there is to know
about one actor. It was just about this time that she received columnist Sidney Fields in her home.

Fields remarked that when they were first married,
Coop was already a big star — and that Rocky has never
known a moment of money worry; whatever else it's been,
it's been an easy life.

"Undeservedly so," commented Rocky, "even with all
the trials and tribulations of marriage. If I'd have married
a nice young man in a gray flannel suit, none of this would
have been possible."

She swept her hand across the huge living room chock
full of lavish appointments.

"We travel," she went on. "We meet the great people of
the world. You can disagree madly with your husband if
he's famous, but he never bores you. And to be bored with
the life you lead is the deadliest boredom."

Then Rocky touched on the nub of their past tensions
and past troubles and talked about it with a remarkable
perspicacity — to add further to the legend of the "amazing" marriage.

"It's healthy for wives and husbands to get a break from
each other," Rocky said. "When he stars in a Western next

month, I'll go to visit my mother in New York, and when he goes to shoot *The Sundowners* next year in Australia, I won't go, though he asked me to."

An equilibrium had been restored to the Cooper marriage at last.

And with that, Coop plunged ahead into picture making with a new zest.

Following *Friendly Persuasion*, he appeared in *Ten North Frederick*, a screen adaptation of John O'Hara's massive best-selling study of a Pennsylvania family, and, in particular, of the tortured hero, Joe Chapin, a wealthy, pedigreed attorney.

In it, Coop portrayed an honorable man who lived by the rules and found himself the victim of his own decency. His death at the end, following an abortive attempt to enter high politics and a bittersweet romance with a girl half his age, played by Suzy Parker, stands as a towering ironic commentary on life.

During the production of *Ten North Frederick*, and for a time after its release, the gossip mills ground out rather colorless little items romantically "linking' Coop and Suzy Parker, a remarkably beautiful redhead who had been America's most highly paid fashion model. But the stories clearly had no foundation, and the columnists soon gave it up as a weary, unfruitful enterprise.

However, in a short time Suzy Parker became an item once again — in big headlines in the New York *Daily News*. The newspaper discovered Suzy and 70-year-old Paul Shields had sailed from his Southampton home on his yacht to an East River pier in Manhattan. The same Paul Shields who was Rocky Cooper's stepfather and Gary Cooper's father-in-law.

It seemed now that Suzy was duplicating the May–December romance she had in *Ten North Frederick*, with big Coop. The story received no comment from Shields, Suzy, or Coop and soon died of suffocation.

Following *Ten North Frederick* — in that same year of 1958 — Coop's next picture was released, and in it Gary was back in his familiar saddle.

Man of the West was generally acclaimed by the critics for what it was, a small but arresting film that made no pretense at grandeur or significance. It was simply a well-spun yarn, well acted, with tight economy, that told of Link Jones, played by Gary, and his return to the prairie killer gang he once belonged to. His mission is to save a girl named Billie Ellis, played by Ruth Roman, from the gang's leader, the sadistic Dock Robin, portrayed by Lee J. Cobb. He does, of course, but not before a pip of a gun fight. One critic summed up the picture by saying, "This is a small picture, but it does have a cryptic defiance and an aura of snakelike evil that gets one."

Satisfied with the picture and the way he handled himself, Coop decided to continue with Westerns. He chose for his next adventure an adaptation of Dorothy M. Johnson's moody long short story, *The Hanging Tree.* His co-star in this one was the extremely talented and lovely Maria Schell. Like *Man of the West, The Hanging Tree* had as its climax a titanic battle, this one between Cooper, playing an austere Montana doctor, and Karl Malden, as a greedy, lecherous gold miner who lusts for Miss Schell.

Then in quick succession Coop appeared in *The Wreck of the Mary Deare*, a sea thriller in which he costarred with Charlton Heston, and *They Came to Cordura*, in which Coop, Rita Hayworth, Van Heflin, Tab Hunter, and Richard Conte found themselves in the deep, barren, sunbaked north country of Mexico in a grueling test of stamina and courage. Both films were given good ratings.

In between his films, Coop managed to fit in a full life

of activity with Rocky and Maria. They'd be off to Sun Valley for some skiing, or to Palos Verdes, or Nassau for a vacation of skin diving. Occasionally their journeying would take them to Europe or, especially during the warm weather, to their Southampton summer home.

Once on a trip to New York, Ira Tulipan, of 20th Century-Fox, came to see Coop and asked if he would be the mystery guest on television's *What's My Line?*

"Oh, they'd know my voice the minute I opened my mouth," Coop said.

"But you can change your voice," Ira persisted, trying to change Coop's mind. "Besides, you will get five hundred dollars for the appearance."

"Tax-free?" Coop bounced back.

"What do you care?" Ira asked. "You're a rich man."

Coop turned to Wanda Hale, the New York *Daily News* movie critic who was listening to the exchange. He shot her one of those Gary Cooper looks of desperation and quipped:

"Girl, if I were a rich man I would do nothing but play golf and hunt for the rest of my life."

Coop went on *What's My Line?* The blindfolded panel had little trouble recognizing him.

Inwardly, Coop was pleased that he was so instantly recognizable, even by a mere peep of his voice.

Coop, then, was finding rich, enduring rewards as he moved from the summer to the autumn of life. He wasn't old, but he was getting on in years, and a good deal of his life was past. For Gary Cooper, it was a time of reflection. Not so much of summing up, as a long look backward to find what, if anything, had been missing, and to take hold of it and bring it with him into the years ahead.

In 1959, he knew what it had to be.

He knew it must be a new nearness to God.

CHAPTER TWENTY

Gary Becomes a Catholic

On April 9,1959, Gary Cooper, an Episcopalian all his life, became a Roman Catholic.

With little of the fanfare that has attended other Hollywood stars who have changed their religious affiliation, Gary Cooper took the vows that brought him into the faith of his wife and daughter. It was accomplished quietly and simply. Only a handful of relatives and friends turned up at the Church of the Good Shepherd in Beverly Hills to witness the ceremony. Even the press handled their coverage of the event decorously. Gary, who had been taking instruction at the church where a number of Hollywood luminaries, including Bing Crosby, were among the parishioners, said little of his conversion at the time.

Rocky commented only that "Gary's very happy about it. It took a long time to make up his mind, but he has finally seen the light."

It wasn't until several months later, when the publicity impact of his conversion had faded, that Coop began to talk of it at length, and then a powerful story of love and devotion unfolded.

The idea of converting to Catholicism had first taken seed in Coop's mind six years earlier, when he was granted an audience with Pope Pius XII during a 1953 visit to Rome.

As the years rolled on, the thought remained with him rather like a flameless but still-glowing ember. Coop's nature itself was the greatest obstacle.

"I'm just not a naturally religious man," Coop said to Hollywood writer Ruth Waterbury in an interview published in *Motion Picture* magazine.

Nor did he try to change overnight, perhaps because the old habits of living were too deeply entrenched. The fabric of his life was so tightly woven that there seemed little room left for innovation of idea or spirit. Coop himself recognized this. During this extraordinarily penetrating interview, Coop said:

"Until I was converted this spring, I'd spent all my waking hours, year after year, doing almost exactly what I, personally, wanted to do, and what I wanted to do wasn't always the most polite thing, either.

"I do know that when I was much younger all I was thinking about was getting myself bigger and better parts and meeting more beautiful and sexier girls. I've had a lot of good things in my life, maybe too many of them. Fame. Success. Money. And of course love. I guess plenty of love.

"My parents were very loving toward me, and since 1933 I've been married to a wonderful girl whom I love very much. We have a wonderful daughter who I think is the nicest young girl I ever met.

"Yes, I've had a lot of love. It's true I've had some of the other — some disappointments, some despair, some worry. I've had some moments of swellheadedness, too, moments of horrible conceit. Maybe that's what happens when you make a go of it in this business.

"People brushing my coat and powdering my face and interviewing me and nine million otherwise sensible people wanting to know what my favorite dish is. That's apt to make you think you're a pretty remarkable, unique fellow.

"But on the whole it's been good for me. And then this past winter I began to dwell a little more on what's been in my mind for a long time. I began thinking, 'Coop, old boy, you owe somebody something for all your good fortune.' I guess that's what started me thinking seriously about my religion."

Coop evidently gave it a good deal of thought. A studio executive recalled Coop staring into a cup of coffee at the commissary and saying, as he nodded his head as though pondering the incredible, "How do you figure it out? Look at me. Look at my career. I never in my wildest dreams ever thought I'd get to become a star. Do you realize I got into this business by accident? No newspaper would hire me as a cartoonist. Now look where I am. I'll tell you something. I figure it's time I try to be at least a half decent sort of person, which is something I've not always been."

Cooper was, of course, being overly self-deprecatory, but he did feel the impulse to add some stability to his life and, perhaps oversimplifying it, "turn over a new leaf."

His wife and daughter were there to help him. Rocky had been born a Catholic and felt strongly about her religion. Maria was deeply religious.

Together the three of them began talking about Catholicism, sometimes casually, sometimes probingly. Some new thoughts entered Coop's mind. Some old doubts left. And then two things happened: One, he began to see value in religion.

"I saw that religion is a sort of checkup on yourself,"

Coop said later, "a kind of patterned way of behaving. As I saw it, if a fellow goes to church, and tries to straighten out his mind, it sure helps."

The other is that he began to view religion in relationship to Rocky and Maria.

"I saw and began thinking," Coop said, "how our family had always done everything together, whether it was traveling around the globe or skin diving, or horseback riding, or what have you. So I thought, 'Why am I not sharing a very important part of their life — religion? Why have I been out of it?' I knew then that I didn't want to be any longer."

Rocky's understanding during all that time was important. Had she tried to push Gary into joining the Catholic Church, very possibly she might have failed. It had to be his own decision. Rocky knew that. Once before, she herself had come face-to-face with a deeply disturbing problem involving religion.

That, of course, was, her separation from Gary in 1950 that lasted nearly two years and led her, finally, in 1952, to agree to a divorce if that was what Big Coop wanted. Because of the Catholic Church's ban on divorce, it was a tremendous decision for Rocky to make, but she made it alone just as she knew Coop alone had to make his decision about the Catholic Church.

Shortly after he and Rocky reconciled, Coop's audience with the Pope took place, and then he began thinking his first thoughts about religion.

"I felt that maybe I was a little wiser than I had been," Coop told Ruth Waterbury. "But part of my being brighter was my realization that, if I wanted to keep on being a better guy, I'd need some guidance."

Over the years the idea grew, and Coop finally made his dramatic move in 1959.

Had he come to any deeper, more lasting convictions about religion and life in general?

Gary Cooper summed up his thoughts.

"Having a faith, being a Catholic," he told Miss Waterbury, "made a big difference to me. I found out you don't have to get all wound up in religion, but the knowledge that it is there, with its rules and its vast storehouse of experience, gives you an inner security. In any faith, you will find a few cranks who have become bigots, but any person can have faith without extremes.

"One thing the lessons teach you is that life is as complex as human beings are complex, and you come to judge people and events with less harshness.

"Take a little thing like the way I used to talk about people behind their backs. I never meant any harm. Mine was the kind of gossip we all indulge in, particularly in Hollywood.

"But next day I'd think, 'Now what the heck did I say that for?' That's sure a small correction to make in my character, but it's an example of the corrections I'm trying to make.

"Another thing religion made me come to appreciate was my luck in getting into a good, clean business, like acting. Oh, I know all the gossip, all the supposed knifing that goes on to get roles and the rest of it, but anybody who really knows the movie business knows that to be a success you don't have to knock somebody else down. If you're lucky enough to have some quality the public likes, you don't have to take anybody's hide off to get ahead. Maybe you don't have to in other businesses either, when you really know the inside of them, but movies are the only trade I know."

Coop concluded his interview with Miss Waterbury with a good-natured laugh and this comment on the discovery of the solidarity religion brings:

"If you think this new attitude comes hard to me, you're crazy. I'll never be anything like a saint, I know. I just haven't got that kind of fortitude. The only thing I can say for me is that I'm trying to be a little better. Maybe I'll succeed."

With a new dimension added to his life, Coop seemed to take on a new drive and new concepts in his work. Except for the early years when he'd occasionally drift away from Hollywood and motion pictures with no care for the consequences, Gary had always taken his profession seriously. Now he became a defender of the art and craft of moviemaking as a whole.

A snatch of conversation a friend from MGM recalled showed Coop's new attitude. Gary told the MGM man while he was shooting *Wreck of the Mary Deare*:

"I was cast in a picture recently with a kid who said she was in the movies 'for a lark.' That made me damn mad at her. You never learn all there is to know about acting. It can't be done. And the public deserves that you don't regard it as 'just a lark.' But if I were to work with that girl again, I think I could reserve judgment, be more tolerant, I guess you'd call it."

If the comfort of religion made Coop more tolerant, it did nothing to blunt his energies. He worked through *Wreck of the Mary Deare*, then moved quickly into *They Came to Cordura*.

And then the ironies of life played out a portion of their hand.

Just when Gary Cooper had come to know a new spiritual strength, a painful physical weakness set in. Coop found he had to curtail his working schedule considerably because of some abdominal trouble.

"Looks like the old machine needs an overhaul," he quipped one day to Rocky. A week later he was in a

Hollywood hospital for abdominal surgery. He was up and around a short while later, but within six weeks he again required hospitalization. He entered a hospital in Boston this time, and underwent major surgery on his prostate gland.

By the end of 1960, though, the resilient Coop, fit again as a six-string guitar, was off to London to undertake a new film, *The Naked Edge.*

One day, as the final sequences of the 95th feature picture he had made in his 36 years in the movies were being shot, Coop walked into his cramped dressing room and hurriedly grabbed a bathrobe to put on over his wet and "bloodied" shirt. Then he paused for a warm cup of tea.

"Seem to have a cold in my back all the time I'm in this country," Gary complained. "I go back to the hotel in the evening. Got a room with a dandy view of the river. I sit there and look at it and the draft hits me. Things are tough all over."

Cooper unlimbered his long legs and talked eagerly of his search for "a really great Western script."

What of *The Virginian* and *High Noon*, his greatest?

"Nope," he replied, "the picture that has been built up of the West is all out of proportion — or perspective. You'd think the West had been opened by a bunch of gunmen with only a sheriff's posse to keep law and order. It was just the reverse."

Then Coop leaped to his feet, cringing a bit at the pain he felt in his back.

"Look," he snapped, "did you ever see anything so idiotic as some of these TV cowboys? Hell, they grab the saddle with the wrong hand when they mount. And they can't ride anyway."

Gary contorted himself into a crouching stance, hands below his knees.

"And look at how they carry their guns, down around their knees somewhere so they can make a production job out of drawing."

Then Coop dropped back into his chair, laughing, but for a moment. His face grew serious again. A thought just occurred to him in his deeply critical mood.

"You know," he said, "there's a scarcity of young name stars. The biggest names today are the disc jockeys and the crooners. This is fine for us old guys.

"But people hang on after they should quit. . . . The urge to act stays with you. Sometimes in the middle of a scene I find myself saying a piece of dialogue from fifteen years ago. Situations tend to repeat themselves, and there's a limit to the things you can do with one face and one carcass. For a while I thought about retiring. Sometimes still do, about 5 in the evening.

"But I'd go nuts."

In life, as in his films, Coop demanded the very best of himself and of others around him. But above all he demanded honesty.

Coop liked being in *The Naked Edge* — he liked the idea behind it.

"It's a whodunit, a good one, I think," he said. "Different sort of thing for me. Problem is to play on the innocent side and still bring out to the audience the circumstances that seem to make me guilty. Well, there's a bigger problem. I don't know whether people will believe that Gary Cooper could commit a crime. For the picture to work, there has to be some believability that he did kill this other fella.

"Going to be interesting to see how it comes out. . . ."

Gary Cooper never did find out.

The film was still being processed when the big guy. . . .

The Final Hours

Possibly Gary Cooper was aware, when he returned to Hollywood from London, that death was riding with him and that it would strike in a matter of months.

He could see the gauntness in his face, watch his already low weight melt slowly from his towering angular frame, feel the terrible pains that wracked his body until strong and merciful drugs took effect.

But to the outside world — to his friends, to his fans, to his vast uncounted public — the explanations for his very apparent illness were glib as he struggled to maintain a brave front.

"Uremic poisoning," he had said at the beginning, and when a cancerous portion of his colon was removed, he called it "an obstruction taken out."

Probably Coop suspected — but he hadn't yet been told, though, that he was going to die of incurable cancer. At a testimonial in his behalf by the Friars Club of Hollywood on January 8, 1961, the gaunt actor wept unashamedly at the outpouring of praise and affection he received, including a tribute from poet Carl Sandburg.

"I want to thank each and every one of you for coming here tonight," Coop said, humbly and sincerely . . . "never has so much fuss been made by so many for so little. . . ."

They laughed when he said it. They cried, some of them, when he said a moment later:

"The only achievement I am really proud of is the friends I have made in this community."

The audience did not know, any more than Coop did, that he was dying. They might have suspected, as Coop suspected. But only three people really knew at that time — the doctor, Rocky, and Maria.

Rocky remembers that it was 4 P.M., December 27, 1960, when she received a call to go to the doctor's office. The doctor had summoned her to break the news about Gary — he had cancer of the lungs, and it was inoperable.

"Now you'll have to enjoy every day," the doctor said, trying to comfort Veronica.

But what comfort was that to Veronica? How could she enjoy every day when she knew that any one day might be the very end? Yet with chin held high, with courage, with determination and grit, Rocky went home to face Coop, a brave smile concealing the utter despair and desolation she felt.

Then in the middle of February, after the Friars fete, Coop returned from a hunting trip in Utah. He was feeling terrible. He looked in Rocky's eyes and, perhaps knowing now without being told, he asked:

"Baby, what do I really have?"

This is what Rocky told author Richard Gehman in an interview for the *American Weekly*.

Rocky then decided she had to tell Coop. She had to

because Gary was running around in a bikini all the time
and was in danger of coming down with pneumonia and,
as Rocky put it, "that would have done it. . . . I could see
him getting pneumonia and going all at once."

How did the big guy take it?

"He did not bat an eye," Rocky told Gehman.

And she remembers the date when she broke the news
to him — February 27. They were getting ready to go to
Florida then.

Coop told Rocky:

"I'm so glad that you let me know."

His voice, according to Gehman, was "heavy with ten-
derness for her, and with embarrassment for making her
suffer on his account."

Despite the gravity of his illness, Coop kept a date in
New York to narrate a television documentary about the
West. He went through agony.

"He would work a few hours and go back to the hotel
and lie down," said Maria.

"And take oxygen," added Rocky.

When they returned to Hollywood, all three knew the
end was approaching.

Rocky also talked about Coop's conversion to Catholicism two years previously.

". . .Oh! Did it stand him in good stead," she said. "Every time he'd receive Communion, he said he felt so much
better. He was completely unafraid of the future. He really
was. No fear whatsoever."

Monsignor Dan Sullivan of the Church of the Good
Shepherd often came to visit during those last days.

Pope John XXIII cabled his own personal, special message to Coop, which cheered him greatly.

And there were books like *Peace of Soul*, by Bishop
Fulton J. Sheen, which Rocky says helped carry her

through the ordeal, and *Seeds of Contemplation,* by Thomas Merton.

"He never lost his sense of humor," Maria said.

As the end drew near, even Coop's courage and concern that others should not worry failed to conceal the ravages of the killer abiding within him.

The first intimation the public had that something was wrong came on April 9 when he was forced to cancel an appointment to tape a guest shot with Dinah Shore for her television show.

A week and a day later, millions across the land sensed that, indeed, something was wrong, desperately wrong, when Cooper failed to appear at the Academy Awards ceremony to accept his special, and third, "Oscar." Jimmy Stewart, Coop's good friend of long standing, weaved his way through the crowd to accept the award on Coop's behalf. Stewart was only able to say, "We're all very proud of you, Coop, all of us are terribly proud" — before his voice broke and he retreated to his seat with tears in his eyes.

By then Coop was confined to his study, a sunny room in the center of the big Holmby Hills house. He was there watching his portable TV set as Jimmy Stewart accepted the award, and it was there, with his stacks of books, with his window facing the beautifully serene garden beyond, that Coop spent the final hours of his life.

Rocky and Maria were at his bedside constantly. For Coop's sake they kept their heads high and did not weep.

No one but his immediate family, his physician, Dr. Rex Kennamer, and his priest, Monsignor Sullivan, could see him.

By the beginning of May, Coop was failing fast. Following the Academy Awards ceremony, because of the massive number of inquiries from the public about Coop's health, Dr. Kennamer began issuing frequent bulletins; but as the days flew by, they were always the same: "Condition, grave."

It wasn't until the final days that pain-killing drugs were given to him.

And Rocky remarked that they could talk to Coop right through "except for the last two days. Then they really put him out, thank God."

Through it all Gary had stood up with courage unwavering.

"It was Gary's faith that made him brave," said Rocky. "I'm certain of that."

Late on the night of May 13, Dr. Kennamer told newsmen gathered at the Cooper house that Gary was sinking rapidly and that death appeared only hours away.

Coop was under heavy sedation and unaware the end was near. The physician said, "There is no hope."

Death came the next afternoon. At 12:47 P.M., May 14, 1961, with his wife and daughter beside him, Gary Cooper passed from this life.

The men and women of the movie colony, the people closest to him in his life and during his sickness, were plunged into a deep personal sorrow. Expressions of sympathy poured in.

From John Wayne: "The world lost its most loved man today."

From Jimmy Stewart: "It's a tremendous loss to so many people that it's hard to put it into so many words. He has meant more to this industry than almost anybody in its history."

From Greer Garson: "A piece is gone from the fabric of all our lives."

From Audrey Hepburn: "By his strength Gary made everyone else stronger. He was a beautiful person."

From Elizabeth Taylor: "It is difficult to say anything. He was so much loved that subconsciously we all tried to ward off his death, trying not to believe it was coming."

But it came. Death finally came. Only the previous November Clark Gable had died at the age of 60, and now, just six days after his own 60th birthday, Gary Cooper, another of the towering giants of the motion picture industry, was gone, too.

And so an era has vanished. Even more than Gable, Gary Cooper represented the early men, the unique men who grew and suffered and changed just as the picture industry itself grew and suffered and changed and contributed so vastly to the dynamism of our incredible century.

Gary Cooper *was* the great shimmering wonderland called "movies" as much as any individual man could be, and with his death, a part, a very vital part, of that world died.

And no new Montana Cowboy, no tall, dust-flecked rider, no loose-limbed, angular hero, no one, can ever quite take his place.

Appendix

GARY COOPER'S FILMS

Dates given are the release dates. (Note: This filmography is not as complete as the author would want it to be. If you can fill in some of the blanks, the author—and all Gary Cooper fans—will be very grateful. All verified information will be added to subsequent editions of this book. Please send your facts to the author, % Arlington House Publishers, 81 Centre Ave., New Rochelle, N.Y. 10801. Thank you.)

As an unbilled extra

THE LUCKY HORSESHOE
(Fox Film Company)

1925.   Producer and director: J. G. Blystone. Story: Robert Lord. Scenario: John Stone. 5 reels. Tinted. *With* Tom Mix.

THE VANISHING AMERICAN
(Paramount)

1925.   Director: George B. Seitz. Screenplay: Ethel Doherty. Adaptation: Lucien Hubbard, from the novel by Zane Grey. 8,916 feet. *With* Richard Dix.

THE EAGLE
(United Artists)

1925.   Producer and director: Clarence Brown. Adaptation: Hans Kraly, from the Russian classic, *Dubrovsky,* by Aleksander Pushkin. 7 reels. *With* Rudolph Valentino, Louise Dresser, Vilma Banky, James Marcus.

THE ENCHANTED HILL
(Paramount)

1925.   Producer and director: Irvin Willat. Screenplay: James Shelley Hamilton and Victor Irwin, from the novel by Peter B. Kyne. 7 reels. *With* Florence Vidor.

WATCH YOUR WIFE
(Universal)

1925.   Director: Svend Gade. Scenario: Charles E. Whittaker and Svend Gade, from the novel by Gösta Segercranz. 7 reels. (Another extra who appeared in this film was Walter Brennan.)

Silent Features

1.   TRICKS
(Davis Distribution Division)

1925.   Produced by Marilyn Mills and J. Frank Glendon. Director: Bruce Mitchell. Story: Mary C. Bruning. *With* Frank Glendon.

2.   THREE PALS
(Davis Distribution Division)

1926.   Produced by Marilyn Mills and J. Frank Glendon. Director: Bruce Mitchell. 5 reels.

3.   LIGHTNING JUSTICE

1926.   Director: Al Nietz.

4.   THE WINNING OF BARBARA WORTH
(*MGM*)

1926.   A United Artists production. Presented by Samuel Goldwyn. Director: Henry King. Adapted by Frances Marion, from the novel by Harold Bell Wright. Cinematographer: George Barnes. 9 reels. *With* Ronald Colman and Vilma Banky. (Cooper's first important role was in this Western. He played Abe Lee.)

5.   ARIZONA BOUND
(*Paramount*)

1927.   Presented by Adolph Zukor and Jesse L. Lasky. Director: John Waters. Story: Richard Allen Gates. Screenplay: John Stone and Paul Gangelin. Adaptation: Marion Jackson, from a story by Zane Grey. 5 reels. *With* Thelma Todd, Betty Jewell, El Brendel, and Jack Daugherty.

6.   NEVADA
(*Paramount*)

1927.   Director: John Waters. Screeplay: John Stone and L. G. Rigby, from the novel by Zane Grey. 6,258 feet. 75 minutes. *With* Evelyn Brent, William Powell, Thelma Todd, and Philip Strange.

7.   BEAU SABREUR
(*Paramount*)

1927.   Presented by Adolph Zukor and Jesse L. Lasky. Director: John Waters. Adapted by Tom J. Geraghty, from the story by Percival Christopher Wren. 6,704 feet. *With* Evelyn Brent, William Powell and Noah Beery.

8.   THE LAST OUTLAW
(Paramount)

1927.   Presented by Adolph Zukor and Jesse L. Lasky. Director: Arthur Rossen. Story: Richard Allen Gates. Adaptation: J. Walter Ruben. Scenario: John Stone and J. Walter Ruben. 6,032 feet. *With* Betty Jewell and Jack Luben.

9.   WINGS
(Paramount)

1927.   Director: William A. Wellman. Story: John Monk Saunders. Screenplay: Hope Loring and Louis D. Lighton. 13 reels. *With* Charles "Buddy" Rogers, Richard Arlen, Clara Bow, and Jobyna Ralston. (Academy Awards: Production, Engineering Effects.)

10.   CHILDREN OF DIVORCE
(Paramount)

1927.   Presented by Adolph Zukor and Jesse L. Lasky. Producer and director: Frank Lloyd. Screenplay: Hope Loring, Louis D. Lighton and Adela Rogers St. Johns, from the story by Owen Johnson. 7 reels. *With* Clara Bow, Esther Ralston, Hedda Hopper and Einar Hanson.

11.   IT
(Paramount)

1928.   Presented by Adolph Zukor and Jesse L. Lasky. Producers: Elinor Glyn and Clarence Badger. Director: Clarence Badger. Adapted by Elinor Glyn, from her novel. Screenplay: Hope Loring and Louis D. Lighton. 6,452 feet. *With* Clara Bow, Antonio Moreno, and William Austin.

12.   THE LEGION OF THE CONDEMNED
(Paramount)

1928. Presented by Adolph Zukor and Jesse L. Lasky. Producer and director: William A. Wellman. Story: John Monk Saunders. Screenplay: John Monk Saunders and Jean de Limur. 7,415 feet. *With* Fay Wray and Lane Chandler.

13.   DOOMSDAY
(Paramount)

1928. Presented by Adolph Zukor and Jesse L. Lasky. Producer and director: Rowland V. Lee. Screenplay: Donald W. Lee, from the book by Warwick Deeping. Adaptation: Doris Anderson. 5,652 feet. *With* Florence Vidor and Lawrence Grant.

14.   THE FIRST KISS
(Paramount)

1928. Presented by Adolph Zukor and Jesse L. Lasky. Producer and director: Rowland V. Lee. Adaptation and screenplay: John Farrow, from the story *Four Brothers,* by Tristram Tupper. 6 reels. *With* Fay Wray, Lane Chandler and Leslie Fenton.

15.   LILAC TIME
(First National)

1928. Presented by John McCormick. Producer and director: George Fitzmaurice. Screenplay: Carey Wilson, based on the play by Jane Cowl and Jane Murfin. Adaptation: Willis Goldbeck. 11 reels. 120 minutes. *With* Colleen Moore and Kathryn McGuire.

16.   HALF A BRIDE
(Paramount)

1929. Director: Gregory LaCava. Screenplay: Doris Anderson and Percy Heath, from the story *White Hands* by Arthur

Stringer. 6 reels. *With* Esther Ralston, Carole Lombard and William Worthington.

17. SHOPWORN ANGEL
(Paramount)

1929. Director: Richard Wallace. Adapted by Howard Estabrook and Albert Shelby LeVino, from the story by Dana Burnet. 8 reels. Sound and silent. *With* Nancy Carroll and Paul Lukas. (Gary Cooper spoke in films for the first time in this picture.)

18. WOLF SONG
(Paramount)

1929. Producer and director: Victor Fleming. Story: Harvey Fergusson. Screenplay: John Farrow and Keene Thompson. 6,070 feet silent; 7,021 feet sound. *With* Lupe Velez and Louis Wolheim.

19. THE BETRAYAL
(Paramount)

1929. Director: Lewis Milestone. Story: Victor Schertizinger and Nicholas Soussanin. Screenplay: Hans Kraly. 6,492 feet silent; 8 reels sound. *With* Emil Jannings and Esther Ralston. (This was Coop's last silent picture.)

Sound Features

20. THE VIRGINIAN
(Paramount)

1929. Director: Victor Fleming. Story: Owen Wister and Kirk LaShelle, based on the novel by Owen Wister. Adaptation: Howard Estabrook. Camera: Edward Cronjager and J. Roy

Hunt. 7,407 feet. 90 minutes. *With* Walter Huston, Richard Arlen, Mary Brian, Chester Conklin, and Eugene Pallette. (Cooper's first all-talkie.)

21. ONLY THE BRAVE
(Paramount)

1930. Director: Frank Tuttle. Story: Keene Thompson. Screenplay: Edward E. Paramore, Jr. 6,024 feet. 71 minutes. *With* Mary Brian and Phillips Holmes.

22. PARAMOUNT ON PARADE
(Paramount)

1930. Supervision: Elsie Janis. Directors: Dorothy Arzner, Otto Brower, Edmund Goulding, Rowland V. Lee, Ernst Lubitsch, Edward Sutherland, Frank Tuttle, *et al.* Choreography: David Bennett. Camera: Harry Fishbeck and Victor Milner. With Technicolor sequences. 9,125 feet. 102 minutes. *With* Jean Arthur, Clara Bow, Maurice Chevalier, Kay Francis, Helen Kane, Fredric March, Jack Oakie, Warner Oland, Lillian Roth, and Fay Wray.

23. THE TEXAN
(Paramount)

1930. Director: John Cromwell. Screenplay: Daniel N. Rubin, from the story *The Double-Dyed Deceiver* by O. Henry. Adaptation: Oliver H. P. Garrett. Film Editor: Verna Willis. 7,142 feet. *With* Fay Wray, Emma Dunn and Oscar Apfel.

24. SEVEN DAYS' LEAVE
(Paramount)

1930. Director: Richard Wallace. Adaptation: Dan Totheroh and John Farrow, from the story *The Old Lady Shows Her*

Medals by Sir James M. Barrie. 7,534 feet. *With* Beryl Mercer, Arthur Hoyt and Daisy Belmore.

25.   A MAN FROM WYOMING
(Paramount)

1930.   Director: Rowland V. Lee. Screenplay: John V. A. Weaver and Albert Shelby LeVino, from a story by Joseph Moncure March and Lew Lipton. 5,989 feet. *With* June Collyer and Regis Toomey.

26.   THE SPOILERS
(Paramount)

1930.   Producer and director: Edwin Carewe and David Burton. Screenplay: Bartlett Cormack, from the novel by Rex Beach. Scenario: Agnes Brand Leahy. 11 reels. *With* William Boyd, Kay Johnson, and Betty Compson.

27.   MOROCCO
(Paramount)

1930.   Director: Josef von Sternberg. Adaptation: Jules Furthman, from the play *Amy Jolly* by Benno Vigny. Film Editor: Sam Winston. Photography: Lee Garmes. 8,237 feet. 90 minutes. *With* Marlene Dietrich, Adolph Menjou, Ulrich Haupt, Juliette Compton, Francis McDonald, Albert Conti, Eve Southern, Michael Visaroff, Paul Porcasi, Theresa Harris. NBR

28.   FIGHTING CARAVANS
(Paramount)

1931.   Directors: Otto Brower and David Burton. Screenplay: Edward E. Paramore, Jr., Keene Thompson, and Agnes Brand Leahy, from the novel by Zane Grey. Film Editor: William Shea. 70 minutes. *With* Lily Damita, Ernest Torrance and Tully Marshall.

29. CITY STREETS
(Paramount)

1931. Director: Reuben Mamoulian. Screenplay: Oliver H. P. Garrett, from a story by Dashiell Hammett. Adaptation: Max Marcin. Photography: Lee Garmes. Sound: J. A. Goodrich and M. M. Paggi. 9 reels. *With* Sylvia Sidney, Paul Lukas, William Boyd, Guy Kibbee, Stanley Fields, Wynne Gibson, Betty Sinclair, Barbara Leonard, Terry Carroll, Robert E. Homans, Willard Robertson, Allan Cavan, Bert Hanlon, Matty Kemp, Edward Le Saint, Hal Price, Ethan Laidlaw, George Regas, Bob Kortman, Leo Willis, and Bill Elliott. *NBR.*

30. I TAKE THIS WOMAN
(Paramount)

1931. Director: Marion Gering. Adaptation: Vincent Lawrence, from the novel *Lost Ecstasy* by Mary Roberts Rinehart. 8 reels. *With* Carole Lombard, Helen Ware, and Lester Vail.

31. HIS WOMAN
(Paramount)

1931. Director: Edward Sloman. Screenplay: Adelaide Heilbron and Melville Baker, from the novel *The Sentimentalist* by Dale Collins. 8 reels. With Claudette Colbert, Douglass Dumbrille, Harry Davenport, and Averill Harris.

32. THE DEVIL AND THE DEEP
(Paramount)

1932. Director: Marion Gering. Screenplay: Benn W. Levy, from a story by Harry Hervey. 8 reels. 78 minutes. *With* Tallulah Bankhead, Charles Laughton, Cary Grant, and Paul Porcasi.

33. MAKE ME A STAR
(Paramount)

1932. Director: William Beaudine. Screenplay: Sam Mintz, Walter DeLeon, and Arthur Kober, from the novel *Merton of the Movies* by Harry Leon Wilson and the play by George S. Kaufman and Marc Connelly. 9 reels.

34. IF I HAD A MILLION
(Paramount)

1932. Directors: James Cruze, Ernst Lubitsch, Norman Taurog, *et al.* Screenplay: Claude Binyon, *et al.,* from the novel *Windfall* by Robert D. Andrews. 9 reels. 88 minutes. *With* Charles Laughton, W. C. Fields, George Raft, Mary Boland, Wynne Gibson, Gene Raymond, Richard Bennett, Charles Ruggles, Alison Skipworth, and Frances Dee. (Cooper, Roscoe Karns and Jack Oakie play Marines who give away $1 million.)

35. A FAREWELL TO ARMS
(Paramount)

1933. Director: Frank Borzage. Screenplay: Benjamin Glazer and Oliver H. P. Garrett, from the novel by Ernest Hemingway. Photography: Charles Bryant Lang, Jr. *With* Helen Hayes, Adolph Menjou, Mary Philips, Jack La Rue, Blanche Frederici, Henry Armetta, George Humbert, Fred Malatesta, Mary Forbes, Tom Ricketts, Robert Cauterio, and Gilbert Emery. (Academy Awards: To Charles Bryant Lang, Jr., for Cinematography, to Harold C. Lewis, for Sound Recording,) NBR. FDA.

36. TODAY WE LIVE
(MGM)

1933. Producer and director: Howard Hawks. Story and dialogue: William Faulkner. Screenplay: Edith Fitzgerald and

Dwight Taylor. Film Editor: Edward Curtiss. 11 reels. *With* Joan Crawford, Franchot Tone, Robert Young, and Roscoe Karns.

37.   ONE SUNDAY AFTERNOON
(*Paramount*)

1933.   Producer: Louis D. Lighton. Director: Stephen Roberts. Screenplay: Grover Jones and William Slavens McNutt, from the stage play by James Hagan. 8 reels. *With* Frances Fuller, Neil Hamilton, and Fay Wray.

38.   DESIGN FOR LIVING
(*Paramount*)

1933.   Producer and director: Ernst Lubitsch. Adaptation and screenplay: Ben Hecht, from the play by Noel Coward. Photography: Victor Milner. Sets: Hans Drier. Music: Nathaniel Finston. 10 reels. 90 minutes. *With* Fredric March, Miriam Hopkins, Edward Everett Horton, Franklin Pangborn, and Isabel Jewell.

39.   ALICE IN WONDERLAND
(*Paramount*)

1933.   Producer: Louis D. Lighton. Director: Norman Z. McLeod. Screenplay: Joseph J. Mankiewicz and William Cameron Menzies, from the story by Lewis Carroll (pseudonym of Charles Lutwidge Dodgson). 8 reels. 90 minutes. *With* Charlotte Henry, Cary Grant, W. C. Fields, Richard Arlen, Edward Everett Horton, Mae Marsh, Edna May Oliver, and Jack Oakie.

40.   OPERATOR 13
(*MGM*)

1934.   Producer: Lucien Hubbard. Director: Richard Boleslavsky. Screenplay: Harvey Thew, Zelda Sears and Eve Greene, from the stories by Robert C. Chambers. Film Editor: Frank Sullivan. 9 reels. *With* Marion Davies, Sidney Toler, Mae Clarke, Walter Long, and the Mills Brothers.

41.   NOW AND FOREVER
(Paramount)

1934.   Presented by Adolph D. Zukor. Producer: Louis D. Lighton. Director: Henry Hathaway. Story: Jack Kirkland and Melville Baker. Screenplay: Vincent Lawrence and Sylvia Thalberg. Music and lyrics: Harry Revel and Mack Gordon. 9 reels. 81 minutes. *With* Carole Lombard, Shirley Temple, Henry Hathaway, Sir Guy Standing, Charlotte Granville, and Harry Stubbs.

42.   THE WEDDING NIGHT
(United Artists)

1935.   Director: King Vidor. Screenplay: Edith Fitzgerald, from an original story by Edwin Knopf. Camera: Gregg Toland. 9 reels. 84 minutes. *With* Anna Sten, Ralph Bellamy, Sig Ruman, and Helen Vinson.

43.   LIVES OF A BENGAL LANCER
(Paramount)

1935.   Presented by Adolph Zukor. Producer: Louis D. Lighton. Director: Henry Hathaway. Screenplay: Waldemar Young, John L. Balderson, and Achmed Abdullah, from the book by Frances Yeats-Brown. Adaptation: Grover Jones and Williams Slavens McNutt. 11 reels. 109 minutes. *With* Franchot Tone, Richard Cromwell, Sir Guy Standing, C. Aubrey Smith, Monte Blue, Kathleen Burke, Colin Tapley, Douglass R. Dumbrille, Akim Tamiroff, Jameson Thomas, Noble Johnson, Lumsden Hare, J. Carroll Naish, Mischa Auer, Leonid Kinsky, and Major Sam Harris. NBR, FDA.

44.   PETER IBBETSON
(Paramount)

1935.   Presented by Adolph Zukor. Producer: Louis D.
Lighton. Director: Henry Hathaway. Screenplay: Vincent Law-
rence and Waldemar Young, from the novel by George Du
Maurier and the play by John Nathaniel Raphael. Adaptation:
Constance Collier, with additional scenes by John Meehan and
Edwin Justus Mayer. Film Editor: Stuart Heisler. Music score:
Ernst Toch. 10 reels. 88 minutes. *With* Ann Harding, John
Halliday, Ida Lupino, Douglass R. Dumbrille, Virginia Weldler,
Dickie Moore, and Doris Lloyd.

45.   DESIRE
(Paramount)

1936.   Presented by Adolph Zukor. Supervision: Ernst
Lubitsch. Director: Frank Borzage. Screenplay: Edwin Justus
Mayer, Waldemar Young, and Samuel Hoffenstein, from a play
by Hans Szekely and R. A. Stemmle. Photography: Charles Lang
and Victor Milner. Music and lyrics: Frederick Hollander and
Leo Robin. 10 reels. Song: "Awake in A Dream." 89 minutes.
With Marlene Dietrich, John Halliday, William Frawley, Ernest
Cossart, Akim Tamiroff, and Alan Mowbray.

46.   MR. DEEDS GOES TO TOWN
(Columbia)

1936.   Director: Frank Capra. Screenplay: Robert Riskin,
from the story *Opera Hat* by Clarence Buddington Kelland.
Film Editor: Gene Havlick. Music Director: Howard Jackson.
12 reels. 115 minutes. *With* Jean Arthur, George Bancroft,
Lionel Stander, Douglass Dumbrille, Raymond Walburn, Mar-
garet Matzenauer, H. B. Warner, Ruth Donnelly, Irving Bacon,
Frank Pangborn, and Dennis O'Keefe. (Academy Award: Frank
Capra, for director; New York Film Critics Award: Best Motion
Picture of the Year.)

47.   THE GENERAL DIED AT DAWN
(Paramount)

1936.   Presented by Adolph Zukor. Director: Lewis Milestone. Story: Charles G. Booth. Screenplay: Clifford Odets. 10 reels. 97 minutes. *With* Akim Tamiroff, Madeleine Carroll, Porter Hall, Dudley Digges, William Frawley, and John O'Hara.

48.   HOLLYWOOD BOULEVARD
(Paramount)

1936.   Presented by Adolph Zukor. Producer: A. M. Botsford. Supervision: Edward F. Cline. Director: Robert Florey. Story: Max Marcin and Faith Thomas. Screenplay: Marguerite Roberts. 8 reels. *With* Pat O'Malley, Freeman Wood, Maurice Costello, Creighton Hale, Charles Ray, Francis X. Bushman, Herbert Rawlinson, Esther Ralston, and William Desmond.

49.   THE PLAINSMAN
(Paramount)

1937.   Presented by Adolph Zukor. Producer and director: Cecil B. DeMille. Screenplay: Waldemar Young, Harold Lamb and Lynn Riggs, from stories by Courtney Ryley Cooper and from *Wild Bill Hickock* by Frank J. Wilstach. Music Director: Boris Morros. Special score: George Antheil. *With* Jean Arthur, James Ellison, Charles Bickford, Helena Burgess, George Hayes, Anthony Quinn, Irving Bacon, Bud Flanagan (Dennis O'Keefe), Porter Hall, and Victor Varconi.

50.   SOULS AT SEA
(Paramount)

1937.   Presented by Adolph Zukor. Director: Henry Hathaway. Story: Ted Lesser. Screenplay: Grover Jones and Dale Van Every. Editor: Ellsworth Hoagland. Original music: Roland

Anderson. Music Director: Boris Morros. 10 reels. 92 minutes. *With* George Raft, Frances Dee, Olymphe Bradna, Henry Wilcoxon, Harry Carey, Robert Cummings, Joseph Schildkraut, and George Zucco.

51.   THE ADVENTURES OF MARCO POLO
(*United Artists*)

1938. Producer: Samuel Goldwyn. Director: Archie Mayo. Story: N. A. Pogson. Screenplay: Robert E. Sherwood. Film Editor: Fred Allen. Music Director: Alfred Newman. Music: Hugo Friedhofer. 11 reels. 100 minutes. *With* Sigrid Gurie, Basil Rathbone, George Barbier, Binnie Barnes, Ernest Truex, Allan Hale, and Lana Turner.

52.   BLUEBEARD'S EIGHTH WIFE
(*Paramount*)

1938. Presented by Adolph Zukor. Producer and director: Ernst Lubitsch. Screenplay: Charles Brackett and Billy Wilder, from a play by Alfred Savoir and the English adaptation by Charlton Andrews. Film Editor: William Shea. Music: Werner Heymann. Photography: Leo Tover. 9 reels. *With* Claudette Colbert, Edward Everett Horton, David Niven, Hermann Bing, Franklin Pangborn, and Sacha Guitry.

53.   THE COWBOY AND THE LADY
(*United Artists*)

1938. Producer: Samuel Goldwyn. Director: H. C. Potter. Screenplay: S. N. Behrman and Sonya Levien, based on an original story by Leo McCarey and Frank R. Adams. Film Editor: Sherman Todd. Music Director: Alfred Newman. 9 reels. 91 minutes. *With* Walter Brennan, Merle Oberon, Patsy Kelly, Fuzzy Knight, and Harry Davenport.

54. BEAU GESTE
(Paramount)

1939. Producer and director: William A. Wellman. Screenplay: Robert Carson, from the novel by Percival Christopher Wren. Film Editor: Thomas Scott. 12 reels. 120 minutes. *With* Ray Milland, Brian Donlevy, Robert Preston, Susan Hayward, J. Carroll Naish, Albert Dekker, Broderick Crawford, and Donald O'Connor.

55. THE REAL GLORY
(United Artists)

1939. Producer: Samuel Goldwyn. Director: Henry Hathaway. Screenplay: Jo Swerling and Robert R. Presnell, from the novel by Charles L. Clifford. Film Editor: Daniel Mandell. Music director: Alfred Newman. 10 reels. 95 minutes. *With* David Niven, Andrea Leeds, Reginald Owen, Kay Johnson, Broderick Crawford, Vladimir Sokoloff, and Henry Kolker.

56. THE WESTERNER
(United Artists)

1940. Producer: Samuel Goldwyn. Director: William Wyler. Screenplay: Jo Swerling and Niven Busch, from the story by Stuart N. Lake. Music score: Dimitri Tiomkin. Cinematography: Gregg Toland. Film Editor: Daniel Mandell. 10 reels. 100 minutes. *With* Walter Brennan, Doris Davenport, Fred Stone, Paul Hurst, Chill Wills, Forrest Tucker, Dana Andrews, and Lillian Bond. (Academy Award: To Walter Brennan, for Best Supporting Actor.)

57. NORTHWEST MOUNTED POLICE
(Paramount)

1940. Producer and director: Cecil B. DeMille. Screenplay: Alan LeMay, Jesse Lasky, Jr. and C. Gardner Sullivan,

from *Royal Canadian Mounted Police* by R. C. Fetherstonhaugh.
Editor: Anne Bauchens. Music score: Victor Young. Song by
Frank Loesser and Victor Young: "Does the Moon Shine
Through the Tall Pine?" 13 reels. 125 minutes. *With* Madeleine
Carroll, Paulette Goddard, Preston Foster, Robert Preston,
George Bancroft, Lynne Overman, Akim Tamiroff, Walter
Hampden, Lon Chaney, Jr., Regis Toomey, Richard Denning,
Robert Ryan, and Rod Cameron.

58.   MEET JOHN DOE
(*Warner Brothers*)

1941.   Director: Frank Capra. Screenplay: Robert Riskin,
from a story by Richard Connell and Robert Presnell. Music
score: Dimitri Tiomkin. Music Director: Leo F. Forbstein.
Choral arrangements: Hall Johnson. Film Editor: Daniel Mandell. Montage effects: Slavko Vorkapich. 14 reels. 135 minutes.
With Barbara Stanwyck, Edward Arnold, Walter Brennan, Spring
Byington, James Gleason, Gene Lockhart, Rod LaRocque, Irving Bacon, Regis Toomey, and Sterling Holloway.

59.   SERGEANT YORK
(*Warner Brothers*)

1941.   Producers: Jesse L. Lasky and Hal B. Wallis. Direc-
tor: Howard Hawks. Original screenplay: Abem Finkel, Harry
Chandlee, Howard Koch, and John Huston, based on the diary
of Sergeant Alvin York. Music: Max Steiner. 14 reels. 134
minutes. *With* Walter Brennan, Joan Leslie, George Tobias,
David Bruce, Margaret Wycherly, Dickie Moore, Ward Bond,
Noah Beery, Jr., Howard da Silva, June Lockhart, and Elisha
Cook, Jr. (Academy Awards: Gary Cooper, Best Actor; William
Holmes, for film editing; National Board of Review Award and
New York Film Critics Award to Gary Cooper, for Best Male
Performance of the year; FDA)

60. BALL OF FIRE
(*RKO*)

1941. Producer: Samuel Goldwyn. Director: Howard Hawks. Screenplay:Charles Brackett and Billy Wilder, from an original story by Billy Wilder and Thomas Monroe. Music: Alfred Newman. Photography: Gregg Toland. Film Editor: Daniel Mandell. 111 minutes. *With* Barbara Stanwyck, Oscar Homolka, Henry Travers, S. Z. Sakall, Tully Marshall, Leonid Kinskey, Richard Haydn, Dan Duryea, Dana Andrews, Mary Field, and Elisha Cook, Jr.

61. THE PRIDE OF THE YANKEES
(*RKO*)

1942. Producer: Samuel Goldwyn. Director: Sam Wood. Screenplay: Jo Swerling and Herman J. Mankiewicz, from an original story by Paul Gallico. Music: Leigh Harline. Song: "Always" by Irving Berlin. Photography: Rudolph Mate. Film Editor: Daniel Mandell. 128 minutes. *With* Teresa Wright, Babe Ruth, Walter Brennan, Dan Duryea, Elsa Jannssen, Ludwig Stossel, Bill Dickey, George Lessey, Jack Arnold, John Kellogg, Dane Clark, Tom Neal, and Ray Noble and His Orchestra.

62. FOR WHOM THE BELL TOLLS
(*Paramount*)

1943. Producer and director: Sam Wood. Screenplay: Dudley Nichols, from the novel by Ernest Hemingway. Music score: Victor Young. Editors: Sherman Todd and John Link. 19 reels. 170 minutes. *With* Ingrid Bergman, Akim Tamiroff, Arturo de Cordova, Vladimir Sokoloff, Katina Paxinou, Duncan Renaldo, George Coulouris, Pedro de Cordoba, Feodor Chaliapin, Yakima Canutt, and Yvonne De Carlo. (Academy Award: to Katina Paxinou, for Best Supporting Actress.)

63.   THE STORY OF DR. WASSELL
(Paramount)

1944.   Produced and directed by Cecil B. DeMille. Screenplay: Alan LeMay and Charles Bennett, based on the story of Dr. Wassell as told by him and also on the story by James Hilton. Music score: Victor Young. Editor: Anne Bauchens. 15 reels. 140 minutes. *With* Laraine Day, Signe Hasso, Dennis O'Keefe, Carol Thurston, Carl Esmond, Paul Kelly, Elliott Reid, Barbara Britton, Doodles Weaver, Ludwig Donath, Richard Loo, Richard Nugent, George Macready, Minor Watson, Irving Bacon, Frank Puglia, and Yvonne De Carlo. FDA.

64.   CASANOVA BROWN
(International)

1944.   Produced and written by Nunnally Johnson, from the play *Bachelor Father* by Floyd Dell and Thomas Mitchell. Director: Sam Wood. Music score: Arthur Lange. Film Editor: Thomas Neff. 8,239 feet. 94 minutes. *With* Teresa Wright, Frank Morgan, Anita Louise, Grady Sutton, Patricia Collinge, Charles La Torre, Edmond Breon, and Irving Bacon.

65.   ALONG CAME JONES
(International)

1945.   Producer: Gary Cooper. Director: Stuart Heisler. Screenplay: Nunnally Johnson, from the novel by Alan LeMay. Music score: Arthur Lange. Film Editor: Thomas Neff. 90 minutes. *With* Loretta Young, William Demarest, Dan Duryea, Frank Sully, Walter Sande, Jan Costello, Chris-Pin Martin, Bob Kortman, Frank McCarroll, Hank Bell, and Chalky Williams.

66.   SARATOGA TRUNK
(Warner Brothers)

1945.   A Hal B. Wallis production. Executive Producer: Jack L. Warner. Director: Sam Wood. Screenplay: Casey

Robinson, from the novel by Edna Ferber. Music Director: Leo
F. Forbstein. Film Editor: Ralph Dawson. 135 minutes. *With*
Ingrid Bergman, Flora Robson, Jerry Austin, Florence Bates,
Thurston Hall, Theodore Von Eltz, Monte Blue, Franklyn
Farnum and Major Sam Harris. FDA.

67.   CLOAK AND DAGGER
(*Warner Brothers*)

1946.   Producer: Milton Sperling, Director: Fritz Lang.
Original story: Boris Ingster and John Larkin, suggested by the
book by Corey Ford and Alastair MacBain. Screenplay: Albert
Maltz and Ring Lardner, Jr. Art Director: Max Parker. Music:
Max Steiner. Music Director: Leo F. Forbstein. Orchestral
arrangements: Hugo Friedhofer. Film Editor: Christian Nyby.
106 minutes. *With* Lilli Palmer, Robert Alda, Vladimir Sokoloff,
J. Edward Bromberg, Helene Thimig, Ludwig Stossel, and Dan
Seymour.

68.   UNCONQUERED
(*Paramount*)

1947.   Producer and director: Cecil B. DeMille. Screenplay:
Charles Bennett, Fredric M. Frank, and Jesse Lasky, Jr., based
on the novel by Neil H. Swanson. Music score: Victor Young.
Editor: Anne Bauchens. 147 minutes. *With* Paulette Goddard,
Howard da Silva, Boris Karloff, Cecil Kellaway, and Katherine
de Mille.

69.   VARIETY GIRL
(*Paramount*)

1947.   Producer: Daniel Dare. Director: George Marshall.
Screenplay: Edmund Hartmann, Frank Tashlin, Robert Welch,
and Monte Brice. Music score and direction: Joseph J. Lilley.
Special orchestral arrangements: Van Cleave. Editor: LeRoy
Stone. 93 minutes. *With* Mary Hatcher, Bing Crosby, De
Forest Kelley, Bob Hope, Olga San Juan, Billy De Wolfe, Ray

Milland, Dorothy Lamour, Barbara Stanwyck, Paulette Goddard, Veronica Lake, Sonny Tufts, Joan Caulfield, William Holden, *et al.*

70.   GOOD SAM
(*RKO*)

1948. Producer and director: Leo McCarey. Screenplay: Ken Englund, from a story by Leo McCarey and John Klorer. Music score: Robert Emmett Dolan. Film Editor: James McKay. 114 minutes. *With* Ann Sheridan, Ray Collins, Edmund Lowe, Ruth Roman, and Joan Lorring.

71.   THE FOUNTAINHEAD
(*Warner Brothers*)

1949. Producer: Henry Blanke. Director: King Vidor. Screenplay: Ayn Rand, from her novel. Music: Max Steiner. Film Editor: David Weisbart. 114 minutes. *With* Patricia Neal, Raymond Massey, Kent Smith, Robert Douglas, Henry Hull, Ray Collins, and Jerome Cowan.

72.   IT'S A GREAT FEELING
(*Warner Brothers*)

1949. Producer: Alex Gottlieb. Director: David Butler. Screenplay: Jack Rose and Mel Shavelson, from a story by A. L. Diamond. Music: Jule Styne. Music Director: Ray Heindorf. Film Editor: Irene Morra. 85 minutes. *With* Dennis Morgan, Doris Day, Jack Carson, Bill Goodwin, and Irving Bacon. (Cooper was one of the Warner stars photographed on the lot in one scene.)

73.   TASK FORCE
(*Warner Brothers*)

1949. Producer: Jerry Wald. Director-Author: Delmer Daves. Music: Franz Waxman. Film Editor: Alan Crosland, Jr.

116 minutes. *With* Jane Wyatt, Wayne Morris, Walter Brennan, Julie London, Jack Holt, Bruce Bennett, Art Baker, Moroni Olsen, and Laura Treadwell.

74. BRIGHT LEAF
(Warner Brothers)

1950. Director: Michael Curtiz. Based on the novel by Foster FitzSimons. 110 minutes. *With* Lauren Bacall, Patricia Neal, Jack Carson, and Donald Crisp.

75. DALLAS
(Warner Brothers)

1950. Director: Stuart Heisler. Screenplay: John Twist. Music: Max Steiner. 94 minutes. *With* Steve Cochran, Raymond Massey, Will Wright, Reed Hadley, Ruth Roman, and Antonio Moreno.

76. YOU'RE IN THE NAVY NOW
(20th Century Fox)

1951. Director: Henry Hathaway. Previously entitled "U. S. S. Teakettle." Based on an article by John W. Hazard. 93 minutes. *With* Jane Greer, Eddie Albert, Millard Mitchell, Lee Marvin, and Jack Webb.

77. STARLIFT
(Warner Brothers)

1951. Director: Roy Del Ruth. 103 minutes. *With* Doris Day, Gordon MacRae, Dick Wesson, Virginia Nelson, Janice Rule, Ruth Roman, Richard Webb, and Don Haggerty. (Coop appeared in a brief sketch with Virginia Gibson and Frank Lovejoy.)

78.   IT'S A BIG COUNTRY
(MGM)

1951. Directors: Charles Vidor, Richard Thorpe, John Sturges, Don Hartman, Don Weis, Clarence Brown, and William Wellman. 89 minutes. *With* Gene Kelly, Janet Leigh, Fredric March, S. Z. Sakall, Van Johnson, James Whitmore, and Ethel Barrymore.

79.   DISTANT DRUMS
(Warner Brothers)

1951. Director: Raoul Walsh. Story: Niven Busch. Music: Max Steiner. 101 minutes. *With* Arthur Hunnicutt, Ray Teal, Richard Webb, Mari Aldon, and Robert Barratt.

80.   HIGH NOON
(United Artists)

1952. Producer: Stanley Kramer. Director: Fred Zinneman. Screenplay: Carl Foreman, based on the story *The Tin Star* by John W. Cunningham. Music: Dimitri Tiomkin. Song: "High Noon" by Ned Washington and Dimitri Tiomkin, sung by Tex Ritter. 85 minutes. *With* Thomas Mitchell, Lloyd Bridges, Katy Jurado, Grace Kelly, Otto Kruger, Lon Chaney, and Henry Morgan. (Academy Awards: Gary Cooper, for Best Actor; Elmo Williams and Harry Gerstad, for Film Editing; Dimitri Tiomkin, for Music; to Ned Washington (lyrics) and Dimitri Tiomkin (music) for the song, "High Noon"; New York Film Critics Award: best motion picture of the year, and to Fred Zinneman for best direction; Photoplay Gold Medal Award to Gary Cooper as best actor of the year.) NBR, FDA.

81.   SPRINGFIELD RIFLE
(Warner Brothers)

1952. Producer: Louis F. Edelman. Director: Andre De Toth. Screenplay: Charles Marquis Warren, based on a story by Sloan Nibley. Music: Max Steiner. 93 minutes. *With* David Brian, Fess Parker, Phyllis Thaxter, Phillip Carey, Lon Chaney, and Paul Kelly.

82.   RETURN TO PARADISE
(United Artists)

1953.   Director: Mark Robson. Based on the book by James A. Michener. 109 minutes. *With* Roberta Haynes, Barry Jones, John Hudson, and Moira MacDonald.

83.   BLOWING WILD
(Warner Brothers)

1953.   Director: Hugo Fregonese. Story and screenplay: Philip Yordan. 92 minutes. *With* Barbara Stanwyck, Ruth Roman, Ward Bond, and Anthony Quinn.

84.   GARDEN OF EVIL
(20th Century Fox)

1954.   Director: Henry Hathaway. Story and screenplay: Frank Fenton. 100 minutes. CinemaScope. *With* Richard Widmark, Susan Hayward, Hugh Marlowe, Cameron Mitchell, and Rita Moreno.

85.   VERA CRUZ
(United Artists)

1954.   Producer: James Hill. Director: Robert Aldrich. Screenplay: Roland Kibbee and James R. Webb, from a story by Bordon Chase. Music: Hugo Friedhofer and Sammy Cahn. 96 minutes. SuperScope. *With* Burt Lancaster, Denise Darcel, Cesar Romero, Sarita Montiel, George Macready, Ernest Borgnine, Morris Ankrum, Charles (Bronson) Buchinsky, and Jack Elam.

86.   THE COURT-MARTIAL OF BILLY MITCHELL
      (*Warner Brothers*)

1955.   Director: Otto Preminger. Story and screenplay:
Milton Sperling and Emmett Lavery. 100 minutes. CinemaScope.
With Rod Steiger, Charles Bickford, Ralph Bellamy, and Eliza-
beth Montgomery.

87.   FRIENDLY PERSUASION
      (*Allied Artists*)

1956.   Produced and directed by William Wyler. Based on
the book by Jessamyn West. 139 minutes. *With* Dorothy Mc-
Guire, Marjorie Main, Anthony Perkins, Richard Eyer, Robert
Middleton, Phyllis Love, Walter Catlett. FDA; NBR.

88.   LOVE IN THE AFTERNOON
      (*Allied Artists*)

1957.   Produced and directed by Billy Wilder. Based on the
novel, *Ariane,* by Claude Anet. 125 minutes. *With* Audrey
Hepburn, Maurice Chevalier, and John McGiver.

89.   TEN NORTH FREDERICK
      (*20th Century Fox*)

1958.   Producer: Charles Brackett. Director: Philip Dunne.
Screenplay: Philip Dunne, from the novel by John O'Hara. 102
minutes. CinemaScope. *With* Diane Varsi, Suzy Parker,
Geraldine Fitzgerald, Tom Tully, Ray Stricklyn, Philip Ober,
Stuart Whitman, Barbara Nichols, and Joe Faye.

90.   MAN OF THE WEST
(United Artists)

1958.   Director: Anthony Mann. Screenplay: Reginald Rose, based on the novel *The Border Jumpers* by Will C. Brown. 100 minutes. CinemaScope. *With* John Dehner, Frank Ferguson, Julie London, Jack Lord, Lee J. Cobb, Arthur O'Connell, and Robert Wilke.

91.   THE HANGING TREE
(Warner Brothers)

1959.   Director: Delmer Daves. Screenplay: Halsted Welles, from the novel by Dorothy M. Johnson. Music: Max Steiner, 106 minutes. *With* Maria Schell, Karl Malden, George C. Scott, Ben Piazza, Virginia Gregg, and Karl Swenson.

92.   THEY CAME TO CORDURA
(Columbia)

1959.   Director: Robert Rossen. From the novel by Glendon Swarthout. 123 minutes. CinemaScope. *With* Van Heflin, Rita Hayworth, Tab Hunter, Dick York, Michael Callan, and Richard Conte.

93.   THE WRECK OF THE MARY DEARE
(MGM)

1959.   Director: Michael Anderson. Based on the novel by Hammond Innes. 105 minutes. CinemaScope. *With* Charlton Heston, Emlyn Williams, Michael Redgrave, Virginia McKenna, Cecil Parker, Alexander Knox, and Richard Harris.

94.   ALIAS JESSE JAMES
(United Artists)

1959.   Director: Norman Z. McLeod. Screenplay: D. D. Beauchamp and William Bowers, based on a story by Robert S. Aubrey and Bert Lawrence. 92 minutes. *With* Bob Hope, Wendell Corey, Ward Bond, Iron Eyes Cody, Rhonda Fleming, Will Wright, Jack Lambert, Fess Parker, Roy Rogers, and Jay Silverheels.

95.   THE NAKED EDGE
(United Artists)

1961.   Director: Michael Anderson. From the story *First Train to Babylon* by Max Ehrlich. 100 minutes. *With* Deborah Kerr, Eric Portman, Diane Cilento, Hermione Gingold, and Michael Wilding.

FDA: Film Daily Award for one of the 10 best pictures of the year.
NBR: National Board of Review Award for one of the 10 best pictures of the year.

Index

(Italicized page numbers refer to the Filmography.)

of Barbara Worth, 62–68; his first contract (Paramount Pictures), 68–70; in *Arizona Bound, Nevada,* 72–74; learning to fence for *Beau Sabreur,* 74–76; shooting *Wings,* 76–77; with Clara Bow in *Children of Divorce,* 78–84; Hedda Hopper launching his romance with Clara Bow, 85–91; in *The Legion of the Condemned,* 92–93; his first talkie, *Shopworn Angel,* 95; his romance with Lupe Velez, 96–100; in *The Virginian,* 101; with Marlene Dietrich in *Morocco,* 106; making two pictures at a time causes his exhaustion and hospitalization, 107; heading to Europe to recuperate, 109; meeting the Countess Dorothy di Frasso, 111; with Claudette Colbert in *His Woman,* 116; his African safari with Countess di Frasso, 117–122; meeting his future wife, Veronica "Rocky" Balfe, 125; Paramount gives him a new contract and $2,500 a week, 126–127; with Helen Hayes in *A Farewell to Arms,* 127–131; falling in love with Miss Balfe, 127–128; courtship of Miss Balfe, 131–133; Miss Balfe gets rid of the countess, 133; his engagement and marriage to Miss Balfe, 134–137; with Marion Davies in *Operator 13;* with Carole Lombard and Shirley Temple in *Now and Forever,* 139; hitting a new acting plateau in *Lives of a Bengal Lancer,* 140; Mrs. Cooper's attitude on being married to Gary, 141–142; as Longfellow Deeds in *Mr. Deeds Goes to Town,* 142–143; his daughter, Maria, is born, 143; Director William Wyler admonishes Cooper for resenting his role in *The Westerner,* 146–147; in Cecil B. DeMille's *Northwest Mounted Police,* 147–148; as the great American yap in *Meet John Doe,* 148; topping the nation's wage earners with $482,821 in 1939, 149; taking the role in *Sergeant York,* 150–155; winning the Academy Award for *Sergeant York,* 157; as Lou Gehrig in *The Pride of the Yankees,* 160–162; with Ingrid Bergman in *For Whom the Bell Tolls,* 165–166; his stand against President Franklin Delano Roosevelt in the 1944 election, 166–169; as a producer-actor, 170–176, romance with Patricia Neal, 179–189; separation from Rocky, 187; in *High Noon,* 191–193; taking another long walk—to Europe, 193–194; he learns he has an ulcer, 194–195; romance with Giselle Pascal, 195–196; dates with Lorraine Chanel, 197; reconciliation with his wife, 197–198; converting to the Roman Catholic faith, 205–210; his bout with cancer, 213–217.

Cooper, Frank James, 11, 13, 14